HISTORY NOTES

Jacqueline Cavalier
Community College of Allegheny County

OUT OF MANY

A HISTORY OF THE AMERICAN PEOPLE
VOLUME II
TEACHING AND LEARNING
CLASSROOM EDITION

FOURTH EDITION

John Mack Faragher
Yale University

Mari Jo Buhle
Brown University

Daniel Czitrom
Mount Holyone College

Susan H. Armitage
Washington State University

PEARSON
Prentice
Hall

Upper Saddle River, New Jersey 07458

© 2006 by PEARSON EDUCATION, INC.
Upper Saddle River, New Jersey 07458

10 9 8 7 6 5 4 3 2 1

ISBN 0-13-219040-0

Printed in the United States of America

CONTENTS

Chapter Seventeen – Reconstruction, 1863–1877

LECTURE NOTES:

Multiple Choice: Choose the response that best completes the statement or answers the question.

1. The 4 million freed African Americans constituted roughly what fraction of the total Southern population after the Civil War?
a. one-half   c. one-third
b. one-tenth   d. one-fourth

2. Which of the following was NOT a consequence of secession, war, and defeat for white southerners?
a. A loss of much of the best agricultural land.
b. The destruction of most of the South's cotton.
c. Physical and psychological devastation.
d. The recognition of social equality for African Americas.

3. The number ten in Lincoln's Ten Percent Plan referred to the percentage of
a. Southern voters who took an oath of allegiance to the Constitution.
b. African Americans permitted to vote in a state.
c. lands allotted to newly freed African Americans.
d. Republican Party members representing each reconstructed state.

4. General William T. Sherman's Special Field Order 15 provided
a. a harsh punishment for captured Confederates.
b. "forty acres and a mule" to freed men.
c. social, economic, and educational institutions for former slaves.
d. land allotments for Federal officers.

5. Johnson's plan for Reconstruction included all of the following EXCEPT
a. pardons to Southerners who swore an oath of allegiance to the Union.
b. the appointment of provisional governors for former Confederate states.
c. immediate voting and civil rights for former slaves.
d. an emphasis on Reconstruction as the province of the executive, not the legislative branch.

6. Which one of the following statements about Radical Republicans is NOT true?
a. Most had a deep belief in equal political rights and economic opportunity.
b. Most saw the federal government as secondary to state government in the remaking of Southern society.
c. Most Radicals were men whose careers had been shaped by the slavery controversy.
d. They argued for republican institutions, free schools, free churches, and free social intercourse in the South.

7. Which one of the following was NOT a provision of the "black codes"?
a. They were designed to restrict the freedom of the black labor force and keep freed people as close to slave status as possible.
b. Laborers who left their jobs before their contracts expired forfeited wages already earned and were subject to arrest by white citizens.
c. Apprenticeship clauses obliged black children to work without pay for employers.
d. They provided the notion of "separate but equal."

8. The Civil Rights Act of 1866 did all of the following EXCEPT
a. bestowed full citizenship on African Americans.
b. overturned the 1857 Dred Scott decision.
c. overturned black codes.
d. defined all persons born in the United States, including Indian people, as national citizens.

9. The Fourteenth Amendment was passed to ensure the constitutionality of the
a. Wade-Davis bill.
c. Civil Rights Act of 1866.
b. Freedmen's Bureau.
d. First Reconstruction Act.

10. The first Reconstruction Act
a. stipulated that any officeholder appointed by the president with the Senate's consent could not be removed until the Senate approved a successor.
b. divided the South into five military districts subject to martial law.
c. deemed the Civil Rights Act of 1866 unconstitutional.
d. allowed Southern states immediate readmission to the Union.

11. Which one of the following states had NOT been readmitted to the Union by 1868?
a. Florida
c. Virginia
b. North Carolina
d. South Carolina

12. All of the following activists were founders of the American Equal Rights Association in 1866 EXCEPT
a. Elizabeth Cady Stanton.
c. Lucy Stone.
b. Frederick Douglass.
d. Susan B. Anthony.

13. By 1880, nearly three quarters of black Southerners became
a. sharecroppers.
c. "redeemers."
b. factory workers.
d. Democrats.

14. One of the greatest changes in gender roles within African American families as a result of emancipation was
a. the assertion of authority by African American men.
b. more women working outside the home.
c. a greater equality between husband and wife.
d. more women designated as head of the household.

15. The first social institution fully controlled by African Americans was
a. the school.
c. the Freedmen's Bureau.
b. the church.
d. the southern Republican Party.

16. The Republican coalition in the postwar South was composed of all of the following groups EXCEPT
a. African American voters.
b. white Northerners called "carpetbaggers."
c. native white Southerners called "scalawags."
d. Democratic Confederate veterans.

17. The most sweeping measure of the Enforcement Acts of 1870 and 1871 was
a. that which provided for federal supervision of voting.
b. that which authorized the president to send in the army in districts that were declared to be in a state of insurrection.
c. the Ku Klux Klan Act of April 1871.
d. that which declared that interference with voting was a federal offense.

18. The first big businesses in America were
a. mining companies.
c. railroad companies.
b. oil companies.
d. steel mills.

19. Which one of the following statements is NOT true of Liberal Republicans?
a. They supported on-going federal intervention in the South.
b. They emphasized the doctrines of classical economics including the law of supply and demand.
c. They were suspicious of expanding democracy.
d. They proposed civil service reform as the best way to counter machine politics.

20. Which one of the following was NOT a result of the Compromise of 1877?
a. Rutherford B. Hayes became president.
b. Additional support for the Fourteenth and Fifteenth Amendments.
c. More money for internal improvements in the South.
d. Support of "home rule" in the South.

Completion: Insert the correct word or phrase to complete the following statements:

1. The agency established by Congress in March 1865 that was charged with providing social, educational, and economic services and protection to former slaves and destitute, white Southerners was the _____.

2. The constitutional amendment ratified in 1870 which stipulated that the right to vote could not be denied "on account of race, color, or previous condition of servitude" was the _____ Amendment.

3. Laws passed by South Carolina, Mississippi, Louisiana, and other states that were designed to restrict the freedom of the black labor force as well as keep the racial caste system in place were the _____.

4. Passed by Congress in the spring of 1866, the _____ gave full citizenship to African Americans.

5. Founded as a Tennessee social club in 1866, the vigilante group that terrorized black people in the South was the _____.

6. The labor system that evolved during and after Reconstruction which represented a compromise between planters and former slaves was _____.

7. Northern transplants to the South, many of whom were former Union soldiers, were called _____.

8. Southern whites who supported the Southern Republican party during Reconstruction were called _____.

9. The act that divided the South into five military districts subject to martial law was the _____.

10. The organization of the Republican Party in Northern cities that became the political voice of freedmen in Southern cities after 1865 was the _____.

True/False: Indicate whether the following statements are true or false.

1. In 1860, the South held 25 percent of the nation's wealth; a decade later it controlled only 5 percent. (T/F)

2. The articles of impeachment drawn against Andrew Johnson resulted in his removal from office in 1868. (T/F)

3. The Fifteenth Amendment guaranteed the right of American men and women to vote, regardless of race. (T/F)

4. The decision in the 1883 *Civil Rights Cases* deemed the Civil Rights Act of 1875 unconstitutional. (T/F)

5. One of the worst outbreaks of class violence in American history occurred throughout Northern cities during the Great Railroad Strike of 1877. (T/F)

Map Questions: Refer to the maps and accompanying information presented in the chapter to answer the following questions.

1. Compare and contrast the maps of the Barrow Plantation in 1860 and 1881. What changes in the lives of black Southerners are reflected in these two maps? (Map 17-2)

2. Label the states in which regions sharecropping most pervasive. How did this new form of labor affect the lives of former slaves? (Map 17-3)

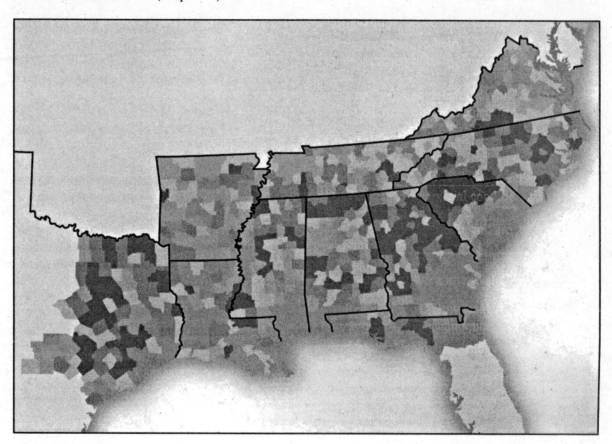

Short Answer Essay

1. How did women's rights advocates respond to the Fourteenth and Fifteenth Amendments?

2. Discuss the emergence of the Ku Klux Klan. How did the federal government deal with the Klan between 1870 and 1872?

3. Identify and define the goals of the major groups that made up the Southern Republicans.

Extended Essay

1. How do the events in Hale County, Alabama, represent the struggles that plagued most communities throughout the South during the era of Reconstruction?

2. What was Abraham Lincoln's plan for Reconstruction and how did it differ from Andrew Johnson's plan? What factors led to the impeachment of Johnson?

ANSWER KEY

Multiple Choice
1. c (434)
2. d (436)
3. a (436-437)
4. b (437)
5. c (438)
6. b (438-439)
7. d (439)
8. d (440)
9. c (440)
10. b (441)
11. c (442)
12. b (443)
13. a (448)

14. a (445)
15. b (446)
16. d (449-450)
17. c (452)
18. c (457)
19. a (458)
20. b (460)

Completion
1. Freedmen's Bureau (437)
2. Fifteenth Amendment (442-443)
3. black codes (439)
4. Civil Rights Act (440)

5. Ku Klux Klan (442-443)
6. sharecropping (448)
7. carpetbaggers (450)
8. scalawags (450)
9. Reconstruction Act (441)
10. Union League (449)

True/False
1. F (435)
2. F (441)
3. F (443)
4. T (454)
5. T (460)

Chapter Eighteen - Conquest and Survival: The Trans-Mississippi West, 1860–1900

LECTURE NOTES:

Multiple Choice: Choose the response that best completes the statement or answers the question.

1. This act dissolved Indian Territory and sovereign status that the Five Tribes did not regain until 1977:
a. Curtis Act.   c. Dawes Act.
b. Morrill Act.   d. Caminetti Act.

2. The area known as No Man's Land was located in
a. the far Western district of Oklahoma.
b. the Eastern Dakotas.
c. Northern Kansas.
d. Central Wyoming.

3. At the close of the Civil War, the majority of Indians in the trans-Mississippi West lived in
a. the Southwest.   c. the Great Plains.
b. Texas.   d. Indian Territory.

4. By the end of the 1850s, how many western reservations had been established by the Bureau of Indian Affairs?
a. five   c. eight
b. two   d. ten

5. Which one of the following brought an end to the Indian Wars?
a. Geronimo's surrender after the Red River War
b. Custer's Last Stand
c. The Sand Creek Massacre
d. The Treaty of Fort Laramie

6. More than any other industry or commercial enterprise, this fostered westward expansion:
a. the railroad.   c. farming
b. mining   d. cattle ranching

7. All of the following statements about early miners' unions are true EXCEPT
a. They fought for the benefit of all workers including immigrants.
b. They were successful in securing legislation mandating an eight-hour work day for certain jobs.
c. They advocated workers' compensation for those injured in the mine.
d. They often retaliated against the mine owners' strike-breaking techniques by sabotaging company property.

8. In the 1879 case of *United States v. Reynolds*, the Supreme Court ruled against the Mormon practice of
a. bigamy.   c. religion.
b. polygamy.   d. theocracy.

9. The "Cortina War" is a good example of conflict over western expansion between
a. open range ranchers and crop farmers.
b. striking miners and their employers.
c. Mexicanos and Anglos.
d. Native Americans and white settlers.

10. Which of the following statements about cowboys is NOT true?
a. Cowboys were paid at best approximately $30 per month.
b. More than one-half of all cowboys were Indian, Mexican, or African American.
c. Cowboys along with miners were among the first western workers to organize against employers.
d. Cowboys offered suffered from scurvy due to the lack of fruits and vegetables in their diet.

11. Which one of the following statements about the Homestead Act of 1862 is NOT true?
a. It was most successful in the central or upper Midwest.
b. It afforded 160 acres of land to any settler who lived on the land for at least two years.
c. Hard-working and adventurous women filed between 5 and 15 percent of the claims.
d. Most settlers acquired land outright rather than filing a homestead claim with the federal government.

12. Most farming families of the Great Plains during the last quarter of the nineteenth century were characterized by all of the following EXCEPT
a. a clear division of labor between men, women, and children.
b. some level of indebtedness to local creditors.
c. the construction of building such as frame farmhouses, barns, and stables
d. the principles of self reliance and isolationism.

13. The federal Hatch Act of 1887 created
a. a series of state experimental stations for basic agricultural research.
b. the Department of Agriculture.
c. land-grants for colleges that promised to institute agricultural programs.
d. the Weather Bureau.

14. From Nebraska to California, the most prosperous crop in the late 1800s was
a. rice.   c. corn.
b. cotton.   d. wheat.

15. Which one of the following species was the most beneficial to the grasslands of the Great Plains?
a. buffalo   c. cattle
b. sheep   d. horses

16. Which of the following acts gave the president the power to establish forest reserves to protect watersheds against environmental threats?
a. The National Reclamation Act of 1902
b. The Timber Culture Act of 1873
c. The General Land Revision Act of 1891
d. The Forest Management Act of 1897

17. All of the following became national parks between 1890 and 1910 EXCEPT
a. Yosemite.   c. Mount Ranier.
b. Crater Lake.   d. Yellowstone.

18. Which one of the following did NOT author a book about the adventures of the West?
a. Theodore Roosevelt   c. Edward Zane Carroll Judson
b. Joseph McCoy   d. Edward L. Wheeler

19. Most reformers' intentions through the reservation policy and the Dawes Act was to
a. preserve Indian culture.
b. curtail white settlement of Indian lands.
c. assimilate tribes into white culture.
d. turn tribes against one another.

20. The Dawes Severalty Act did all of the following EXCEPT
a. successfully assimilated Indians with little resistance.
b. allowed individuals who were legally "severed" from their tribes to petition the U.S. government for citizenship.
c. undermine tribal sovereignty.
d. ban Indian religions and sacred ceremonies and forbid traditional practices.

Completion: Insert the correct word or phrase to complete the following statements:

1. The treaty which acknowledged U.S. defeat in the Great Sioux War in 1868 and guaranteed the Sioux land and hunting rights in South Dakota was _____.

2. The 1864 near annihilation of Black Kettle's Cheyenne band by the Colorado volunteers was the
_____.

3. Meaning "pierced nose," the tribe that was given their name by French Canadian fur trappers was the_____.

4. The 1893 act that gave the state power to regulate the mines was the
_____.

5. The 1882 act passed by Congress which disenfranchised those who believed in or practiced polygamy was the _____.

6. The organization that was formed to protect and fight for the rights of Spanish Americans through political action was the _____.

7. The 1862 act which granted 160 acres of land to any settler who lived on the land for five years and improved it was the _____.

8. The 1902 act which added one million acres of irrigated land to the United States was the
_____.

9. Passed by Congress in 1887, the act that allowed the president to distribute land not to tribes but to individuals legally "severed" from their tribes was the _____.

10. One of the most influential critics of government policy toward the Indian peoples was
_____ who published *A Century of Dishonor* in 1881.

True/False: Indicate whether the following statements are true or false.

1. The purchase of Alaska in 1867 added an area half the size of Texas to the United States. (T/F)

2. Crimes in the West such as horse theft and cattle rustling were typically punishable by lynching. (T/F)

3. The Bon Homme colony of South Dakota was established in 1874 by the German Hutterites who rejected the notion of private property. (T/F)

4. Yellowstone was named the first national park in 1872. (T/F)

5. "Indian schools" attempted to preserve Indian culture by encouraging the use of Indian languages, clothing styles, and hair fashions. (T/F)

Map Questions: Refer to the maps and accompanying information presented in the chapter to answer the following questions.

1. Locate and label by state the locations of Indian reservations between 1860 and 1900 and the names of the tribe(s) that occupied the reservation. (Map 18-1)

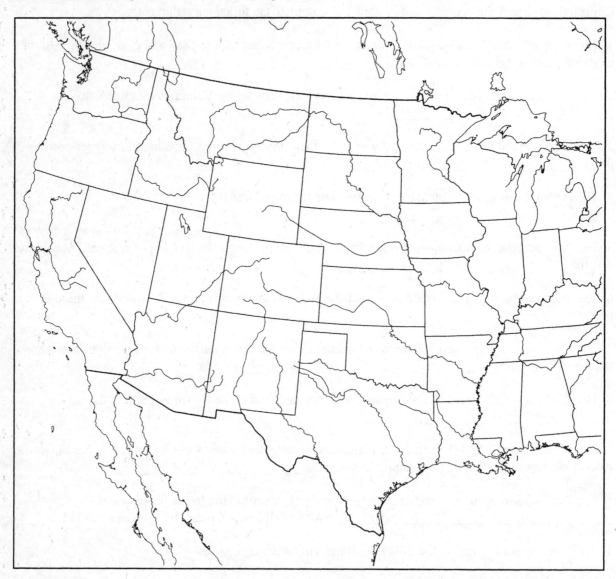

2. Locate and label at least five national forests and the states in which they were established prior to 1930. In which states are the National Parks located? (Map 18-4)

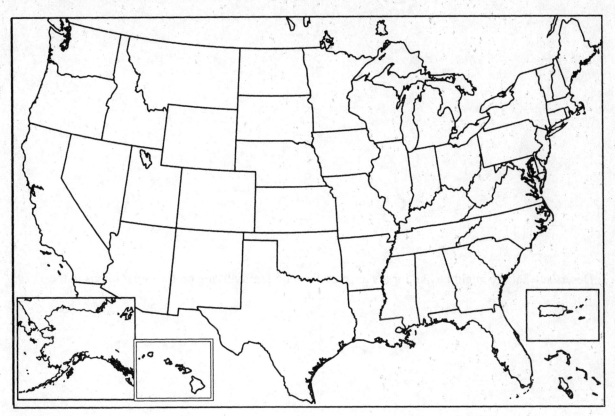

Short Answer Essay

1. What was life like in a nineteenth-century mining town and what kinds of people might you encounter there?

2. Describe what life might be like for the average farming family living on the Great Plains in the 1870s.

3. How did the slaughter of the buffalo affect the Plains Indians?

Extended Essay

1. Describe the various Indian people that populated the West and how the incorporation of Indian territories into the United States affected their nations. Explain as well the causes and consequences of the Indian Wars and the significance of Indian policy including the Dawes Severalty Act.

2. Discuss the response of writers, artists, photographers, and conservationists to the changes that were taking place in the West. What types of stereotypical images of the "Wild West" were presented and how did people of the East react to those images?

ANSWER KEY

Multiple Choice
1. a (468)
2. a (468)
3. c (470)
4. c (471)
5. a (473)
6. b (475)
7. a (477)
8. b (478)
9. c (480)
10. b (481)
11. b (482)
12. d (484-485)
13. a (486-487)
14. d (487)
15. a (488)
16. c (489)
17. d (490)
18. b (490-491)
19. c (492-493)
20. a (493)

Completion
1. Treaty of Fort Laramie (473)
2. Sand Creek Massacre (473)
3. Nez Percé (474)
4. Caminetti Act (477)
5. Edmunds Act of 1882 (478)
6. Hispanic-American Alliance (480)
7. Homestead Act (482-483)
8. National Reclamation Act (489)
9. Dawes Severality Act (493)
10. Helen Hunt Jackson (493)

True/False
1. F (469)
2. T (482)
3. T (484)
4. T (490)
5. F (493)

Chapter Nineteen - The Incorporation of America, 1865–1900

LECTURE NOTES:

Multiple Choice: Choose the response that best completes the statement or answers the question.

1. Which one of the following industries was Chicago's largest manufacturing employer by 1890?
a. steel
b. iron
c. meatpacking
d. railroad

2. A major force behind the economic growth of the last quarter of the nineteenth century was
a. electricity
b. the transcontinental railroad
c. the automobile
d. the telephone

3. By 1900, the United States was _____ in the world in terms of productivity.
a. first
b. second
c. third
d. fourth

4. Rural and urban consumers were drawn into a common marketplace by
a. the automobile.
b. the transcontinental railroad.
c. chain stores.
d. the mail-order house.

5. The United Fruit Company was to vertical integration as this company was to horizontal integration:
a. United States Steel
b. Sears and Roebuck
c. Standard Oil Company
d. American Tobacco

6. The pioneer of scientific management, which advocated taking all of the important decisions out of the hands of workmen was
a. Andrew Carnegie
b. Thorstein Veblen
c. J.P. Morgan
d. Frederick Winslow Taylor

7. African Americans and immigrant women worked mostly in
a. skilled labor jobs.
b. domestic service.
c. clerical positions.
d. sales positions.

8. The Knights of Labor endorsed all of the following measures of reform EXCEPT
a. child labor reform.
b. a graduated income tax.
c. health insurance.
d. an eight-hour work day.

9. The Haymarket Square incident in 1886
a. helped fill the ranks of the Knights of Labor and the AFL.
b. succeeded in gaining more support for the eight-hour work day.
c. weakened the existing wage system.
d. caused a setback for labor unions, especially the Knights of Labor.

10. Which of the following groups were mostly likely members of the AFL?
a. highly skilled wage earners
b. women
c. racial minorities and immigrants
d. unskilled workers

11. The first factory fully equipped with electricity was located in the
a. North.
b. South.
c. East.
d. West.

12. By the 1920s, most of the South's wealth was controlled by
a. former plantation owners.
b. former slaves.
c. northern investors.
d. southern entrepreneurs.

13. The Southern "good roads movement" relied chiefly on
a. convict labor.
b. child labor.
c. immigrant labor.
d. Civil War veterans.

14. Mill superintendents looked mainly to this group to encourage thrift, temperance, and hard work among workers:
a. union leaders.
b. women.
c. community ministers.
d. school teachers.

15. The major source of urban population growth in the late nineteenth century came from
a. African Americans from the South.
b. rural workers from the Midwest.
c. immigrants and their children.
d. native industrial workers.

16. One of the highest population densities in the world in 1890 could be found in
a. Chicago.
b. London.
c. Philadelphia.
d. New York.

17. Mass transportation such as streetcars and trolleys did all of the following EXCEPT
a. eliminate waste from horse carriages that fouled city streets.
b. increase congestion and created new safety hazards.
c. improve the quality of life in American cities.
d. make it possible for workers to live in communities away from their place of work.

18. Examples of the ostentatious wealth and leisure activities associated with the Gilded Age could be found in
a. Newport, Rhode Island.   c. tenement houses.
b. Piedmont communities.   d. company towns.

19. Which one of the following was a member of the new middle class in the late nineteenth century?
a. small business owner   c. engineer
b. lawyer   d. teacher

20. The group that benefited the most from the expansion of American education in late nineteenth century was
a. African American men.   c. immigrant boys.
b. working-class boys.   d. white women.

Completion: Insert the correct word or phrase to complete the following statements:

1. Standard Oil Company is an example of _____, which entails the merger of competitors in the same industry.

2. The philosophy of industrialists such as Andrew Carnegie who preached that hard work and perseverance lead to wealth was called the _____.

3. Passed by Congress in 1882, the _____ suspended Chinese immigration, and also limited the civil rights and forbade the naturalization of resident Chinese.

4. Terence V. Powderly led the _____, which sought to bring together all workers, regardless of skill.

5. Under the leadership of American Federation of Labor president _____, union membership was refused to unskilled workers, racial minorities, women, and immigrants.

6. Once common in New York, the typically overcrowded, four- to six-story residential dwellings that provided minimal ventilation and light were called _____.

7. Thorstein Veblen coined the term _____, which suggested that the rich engaged in highly visible and outward displays of wealth.

8. Mark Twain applied the label _____ to late nineteenth-century America to refer to the shallow display of worship of the wealth that characterized the period.

9. An advocate of practical instruction for African Americans, _____ founded Tuskegee Institute in Alabama to provide industrial education and moral uplift.

10. The _____ was founded in 1877 and offered a variety of courses to Boston's wage-earning women, ranging from foreign languages to dressmaking.

True/False: Indicate whether the following statements are true or false.

1. The 1890 Sherman Antitrust Act succeeded in preventing the consolidation of business and the dominance of industrial giants. (T/F)

2. Southern mill workers earned as little as 12 cents per hour in the 1880s. (T/F)

3. In the 1880s, nearly one-half of all Italian, Greek, and Serbian immigrant men returned to their native countries. (T/F)

4. Two symbols of the new middle-class status in America were the bicycle and the piano. (T/F)

5. By 1910, women constituted more than 50 percent of undergraduate enrollments in American colleges and universities. (T/F)

Map Questions: Refer to the maps and accompanying information presented in the chapter to answer the following questions.

1. Where the chief manufacturing centers located in 1900? Locate and label the areas where coal mining was dominant. Where were the majority of iron and steel mills located? Identify on the map the geographic area known as the Piedmont region. (Map 19-1)

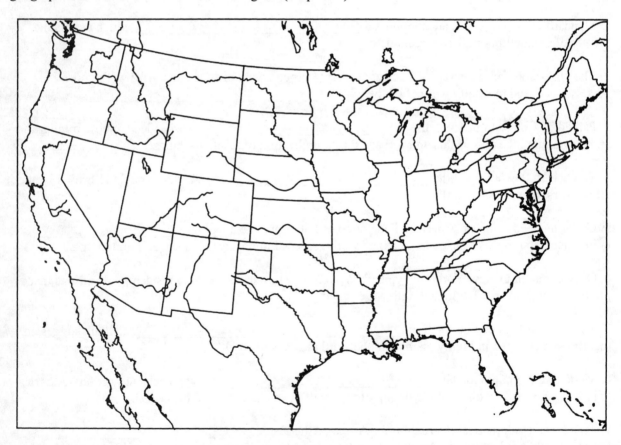

2. Where were the highest concentrations of immigrants in 1880? Outline the areas least populated by immigrants. Identify the settlement patterns of various groups of foreign-born residents in the different regions of the United States in 1900 (i.e., Bohemians, French Canadians, Cubans, and Italians). Why did immigrants tend to settle in some regions and not in others? (Map 19-2)

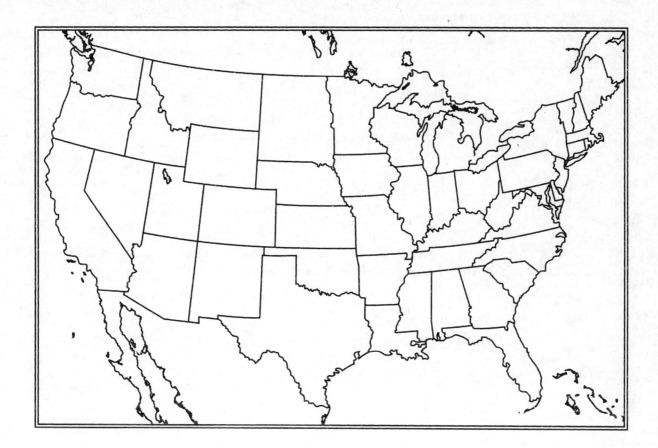

Short Answer Essay

1. Describe life in Packingtown, Chicago, Illinois in the latter part of the nineteenth century.

2. Discuss the role of African Americans in the "New South."

3. Compare and contrast the Knights of Labor and the American Federation of Labor. What were the successes and failures of each?

Extended Essay

1. What factors facilitated the rise of industry and the "triumph" of business by the turn of the twentieth century? What changes occurred in marketing and merchandising?

2. Discuss the experience of the "new" immigrants. What advantages did the close quarters of urban neighborhoods afford the immigrants? What were the disadvantages? Why did immigrants tend to cluster with people of similar ethnic backgrounds?

ANSWER KEY

Multiple Choice
1. c (504)
2. b (505)
3. a (505)
4. d (507)
5. c (508)
6. d (510)
7. b (510)
8. c (511-512)
9. d (512)
10. a (512)
11. b (513)
12. c (513)
13. a (515)
14. c (515)
15. c (516)
16. d (518)
17. c (519)
18. a (521)
19. c (521)
20. d (524)

Completion
1. horizontal combination (508)
2. "gospel of wealth" (509)
3. Chinese Exclusion Act (510)
4. Knights of Labor (511)
5. Samuel Gompers (512)
6. tenements (518)
7. "conspicuous consumption" (520)
8. "Gilded Age" (520)
9. Booker T. Washington (524-525)
10. Women's Education and Industrial Union (524)

True/False
1. F (508)
2. T (514)
3. T (516)
4. T (521)
5. F (524)

Chapter Twenty - Commonwealth and Empire, 1870–1900

LECTURE NOTES:

Multiple Choice: Choose the response that best completes the statement or answers the question.

1. The nineteenth century's bestselling novel after Harriet Beecher Stowe's Uncle Tom's Cabin was
a. Henry George's *Progress and Poverty.*
b. Edward Bellamy's *Looking Backward.*
c. Andrew Carnegie's *Gospel of Wealth.*
d. Josiah Strong's *Expansion.*

2. Which one of the following was NOT one of Edward Bellamy's concepts in his novel *Looking Backward*?
a. Automated machinery will eliminate most menial tasks.
b. The United States would be a cooperative commonwealth.
c. Communities collectively own businesses.
d. The workday would be eight hours long.

3. Which one of the following federal government agencies had NOT been established by 1880?
a. Department of the Interior
b. Department of Agriculture
c. Department of the Treasury
d. Interstate Commerce Commission

4. Which one of the following United States presidents served two non-concurrent terms in the last quarter of the nineteenth century?
a. Grover Cleveland
b. James A. Garfield
c. Chester A. Arthur
d. Benjamin Harrison

5. From 1877 to 1893, the position of the president of the United States was basically
a. a weak position, yielding to Congress and state legislatures.
b. a powerful position, directing Congress and the Courts.
c. powerful in foreign policy, but weak in domestic affairs.
d. well established as a position of representing the "forgotten American."

6. The Pendleton Reform Act attempted to reform what area?
a. civil rights
b. railroad rates
c. civil service
d. public education

7. Grangers were concerned with all of the following EXCEPT
a. American farm equipment being sold more cheaply in Europe than in the United States.
b. finding viable candidates for political office and gaining control of local legislatures.
c. railroad companies and banks that charged exorbitant fees for service.
d. price fixing policies of grain wholesalers, warehousers, and operators of grain elevators.

8. The Great Uprising of 1877 is an example of
a. white laborers against African Americans and immigrants.
b. nationwide farmers' alliances against government and big business.
c. women suffragists against the government.
d. striking laborers against the railroad corporations.

9. If you were a member of the largest organization of women in the world in the late nineteenth century, you belonged to the
a. Women's Christian Temperance Union.
b. Young Women's Christian Association.
c. National American Woman Suffrage Association.
d. National Women's Alliance.

10. Which of the following was NOT a measure included in the People's Party platform?
a. Government ownership of railroads, banks, and telegraph lines.
b. An end to federal income tax.
c. An eight-hour workday.
d. Immigration restriction.

11. The financial collapse and depression of the 1890s was precipitated by the downfall of this company:
a. United States Steel.
b. Standard Oil Refineries.
c. Union Pacific Railroad.
d. Philadelphia and Reading Railroad.

12. The most powerful union in the American Federation of Labor in 1892 was the
a. United Mineworkers Union.
b. Amalgamated Iron, Steel and Tin Workers.
c. American Railway Union.
d. Congress of Industrial Workers.

13. Support for striking Pullman workers in 1894 was especially strong in
a. Western states.
b. the South.
c. the North.
d. New England states.

14. All of the following statements about the Social Gospel movement are true EXCEPT
a. Women played key roles in guiding the movement in their communities.
b. It spread most rapidly in Northern industrial cities.
c. Catholics joined the movement in larger numbers than Protestants.
d. It was formed largely by ministers who called for civil service reform, an end to child labor, and support for labor's right to organize.

15. The "Crime of '73" referred to
a. the elimination of silver from circulation as a result of the Coinage Act.
b. striking railway workers halting train traffic by pulling up rails.
c. poll taxes designed to prevent poor white Southerners from voting.
d. corruption in Grover Cleveland's administration.

16. Both nativism and Jim Crow laws were based on
a. a belief in white supremacy.
b. anti-immigrant feelings
c. the support of social equality.
d. the legal inferiority of African Americans.

17. Which of the following statements about the Good Neighbor Policy is NOT true?
a. It was spearheaded by Secretary of State James Blaine.
b. It allowed U.S. domination in the local economies of Central America and the Caribbean.
c. It involved the expansion of the U.S. Navy to help enforce control of Latin American states.
d. National business classes in Latin America often benefited from the presence of American investors in the economy.

18. Which of the following was NOT an area acquired by 1900 by the United States as a result of American imperialism?
a. Puerto Rico.   c. Panama.
b. Philippines.   d. Hawaii.

19. All of the following statements are true of the Platt Amendment EXCEPT
a. the U.S. acquired territory for a military base in Cuba.
b. the U.S. gained the right to intervene at any time to protect its interests in Cuba.
c. it acknowledged Cuba as a sovereign nation.
d. its conditions contributed to anti-American sentiments among Cuban nationalists.

20. Which of the following individuals is least likely to be a member of the Anti-Imperialists League?
a. Theodore Roosevelt.   c. William Jennings Bryan.
b. Andrew Carnegie.   d. Mark Twain.

Completion: Insert the correct word or phrase to complete the following statements:

1. Created in 1887 to expand federal power over the growing patchwork of state laws concerning railroads, the nation's first independent regulatory agency was the

_____.

2. A major third political party of the 1890s formed by farmers and workers was the

_____.

3. The women's organization whose members preached total abstinence from alcohol consumption was the_____.

4. The idea that the government should expand the money supply by purchasing and coining all the silver offered to it was referred to as _____.

5. Segregation laws that became widespread in the South during the 1890s were called

_____.

6. The "separate but equal" doctrine was established in the 1896 case of

_____.

7. The president of the American Railway Union who ordered a nationwide boycott against the Pullman Company was _____.

8. The organization formed by mine owners in response to the formation of labor unions was the

_____.

9. In his bestselling 1879 book, _____Henry George advocated a sweeping tax on all property to generate enough revenue to allow all Americans to live in comfort.

10. The first nationwide work stoppage in American history occurred in 1877 during the

_____.

True/False: Indicate whether the following statements are true or false.

1. The world's largest women's organization in the 1890s was the Women's Christian Temperance Union. (T/F)

2. William Jennings Bryan was the candidate for both the Populists and the Democratic Party in the election of 1896. (T/F)

3. The Dingley Tariff of 1897 dramatically reduced import duties in the United States. (T/F)

4. Between 1882 and 1900, racial violence declined in the United States, as reflected in the number of lynchings which was less than 100 per year. (T/F)

5. Pope Leo XIII endorsed the right of workers to form trade unions in his 1891 encyclical *Rerum Novarum*. (T/F)

Map Questions: Refer to the maps and accompanying information presented in the chapter to answer the following questions.

1. Locate and label the three states had the greatest number of strikes after the Great Uprising of 1877. What might account for the high concentrations of strikes throughout this region? Which general areas had the lowest number of strikes and why? (Map 20-1)

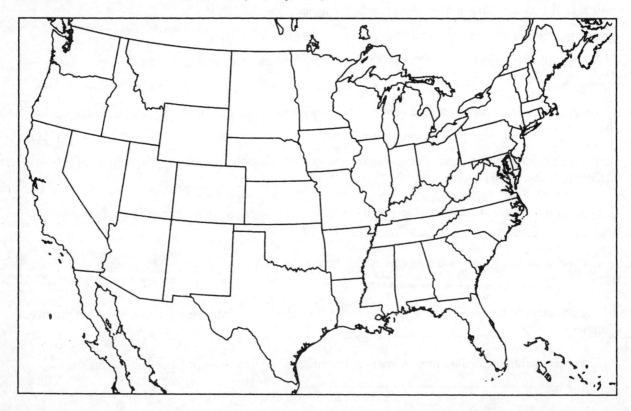

2. Identify in chronological order the islands throughout the South Pacific that had been claimed by the United States by 1900. In what areas throughout Latin America was the United States involved by 1900? (Map 20-3)

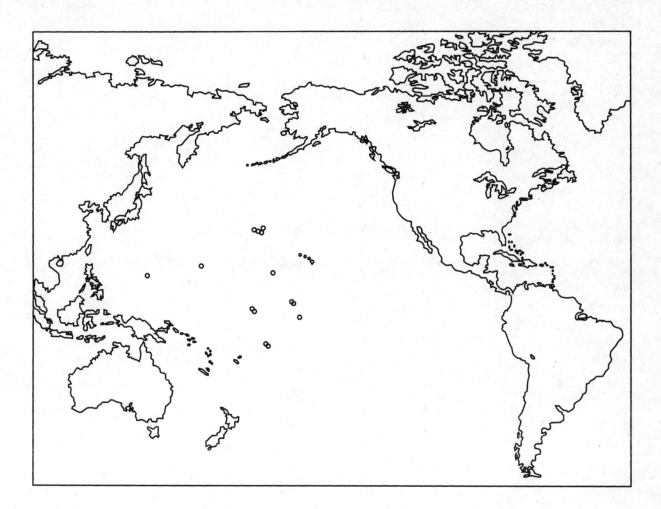

Short Answer Essay

1. What are the key concepts in Edward Bellamy's *Looking Backward* and how was the community of Point Loma a reflection of those concepts?

2. What types of activism were women involved in during the last quarter of the nineteenth century?

3. Compare and contrast two labor strikes that occurred during the last quarter of the nineteenth century. What were the successes and failures of each?

Extended Essay

1. Discuss the role of the Farmer's Alliance and the Grange in respect to the formation of the People's Party. What were the goals of the Populists and how successful were they in achieving their goals?

2. Address American expansionism during the last quarter of the nineteenth century using specific examples such as the Spanish-American War, the annexation of Hawaii, and the war in the Philippines. In what ways did American imperialism contradict the country's founding ideals and how was expansionism made legitimate in light of this contradiction?

Multiple Choice
1. b (532)
2. d (532)
3. d (533)
4. a (534)
5. a (534)
6. c (535)
7. b (535-536)
8. d (537)
9. a (538)
10. b (539)
11. d (540)
12. b (540-541)
13. a (542)

14. c (543)
15. a (544)
16. a (546)
17. d (550)
18. c (551-554)
19. c (554)
20. a (555)

Completion
1. Interstate Commerce Commission (533)
2. Populist Party (535)
3. Women's Christian Temperance Union (538)

4. Free Silver (544)
5. Jim Crow Laws (546)
6. *Plessy v. Ferguson* (546)
7. Eugene V. Debs (542)
8. protective association (540)
9. *Progress and Poverty* (538)
10. Great Uprising (537)

True/False
1. T (538)
2. T (544-545)
3. F (545)
4. F (547)
5. T (543)

Chapter Twenty-One - Urban America and the Progressive Era, 1900–1917

LECTURE NOTES:

Multiple Choice: Choose the response that best completes the statement or answers the question.

1. All of the following statements are true of settlement houses EXCEPT
a. They were reform communities run by college-educated women.
b. They were located in the midst of the neighborhoods they were trying to help.
c. They grew from six in 1891 to 400 houses by 1910.
d. They were progressive, but often anti-immigrant.

2. Which one of the following is NOT an underlying attitude that influenced the emergence of the progressive movement?
a. Universal support for social Darwinism.
b. An emphasis on social cohesion instead of individualism.
c. Anger over the excesses of industrial capitalism and urban growth.
d. A belief in citizen involvement, both politically and morally, to improve social conditions.

3. Which one of the following women is NOT properly matched with her work?
a. Lillian Wald/Henry Street Settlement
b. Jane Addams/Hull House Settlement
c. Ida Tarbell/*Shame of the Cities*
d. Florence Kelley/National Consumers' League

4. George Plunkitt of Tammany Hall called this "honest graft":
a. Working to rid society of social evils such as alcohol consumption, gambling, and prostitution.
b. Making money from inside information on public improvements.
c. Delivering essential services to immigrant communities and business elites.
d. Making money through investments in new economic opportunities such as the movie business.

5. Promoted by Governor Robert M. La Follette, the "Wisconsin Idea" was a way of
a. strengthening direct democracy with direct primaries and other political reforms.
b. controlling large industry.
c. increasing efficiency and social welfare.
d. applying academic scholarship and theory to the needs of the people.

6. Labeled "muckrakers" by Theodore Roosevelt, these people were
a. writers who exposed details of social and political evils.
b. corrupt political bosses in big city machines.
c. pessimists who did not accept the progressive idea of reform.
d. women radicals who wanted more than suffrage reform.

7. In Jacob Riis's book *How the Other Half Lives*, the "other half" referred to the lives of
a. women.
b. African Americans.
c. the urban poor.
d. industrial magnates.

8. Upton Sinclair's novel, *The Jungle*, contributed to the passage of which one of the following laws?
a. The Hepburn Act
b. The Mann Act
c. The Meat Inspection Act
d. The Clayton Anti-Trust Act

9. Which of the following statements about the Anti-Saloon League is least true?
a. It successfully played on anti-immigrant sentiments to garnish support.
b. The energies of the organization were as well put into non-temperance activities such as prison reform and women's suffrage.
c. It drew much of its financial support from local businessmen.
d. It began by organizing local campaigns in which rural counties and small towns banned alcohol within their geographical limits.

10. Which one of the following is NOT a reason that immigrants left southern and eastern Europe to come to America?
a. increased death rates due to disease
b. a shortage of land
c. religious and political persecution
d. growth of commercial agriculture

11. Which of the following immigrant groups were prevented by law from obtaining American citizenship?
a. Mexicans
b. Russian Jews
c. Italians
d. Japanese

12. Which one of the following was NOT a demand of the striking New York garment workers in 1909?
a. union recognition
b. better wages
c. medical benefits
d. safe and sanitary working conditions

13. All of the following statements about the Industrial Workers of the World (IWW) are true EXCEPT
a. Immigrants and unskilled workers were barred from membership.
b. The organization stressed the power of collective direct action such as strikes and sabotage.
c. The union was scorned by other organizations such as the AFL.
d. The leader of the IWW was "Big Bill" Haywood.

14. The publisher of the *Woman Rebel* who coined the term "birth control" was
a. Jane Addams.
b. Margaret Sanger.
c. Florence Kelley.
d. Josephine Lowell.

15. All of the following are credited to W.E.B. Du Bois EXCEPT
a. the Niagara Movement.
b. NAACP.
c. Tuskegee Institute.
d. first African American to receive a Ph.D.

16. Theodore Roosevelt's progressive philosophy did NOT include the belief that
a. centralization was a fact of modern economic life.
b. the government needed to regulate the natural environment.
c. wealthy Americans had a right to use their money and power however they pleased.
d. the persuasive power of the presidency could be used to guide public opinion.

17. Which one of the following political parties did not have a candidate in the election of 1912?
a. the Socialist Party
b. the Progressive Party
c. the Republican Party
d. the Populist Party

18. Which one of the following is NOT a reason that the election of 1912 was the first "modern" presidential race?
a. It featured the first direct primaries.
b. Candidates avoided issues and engaged in "mud slinging" instead.
c. Traditional loyalties were challenged.
d. There was a high degree of interest group activity.

19. All of the following were passed in Wilson's first term in office EXCEPT the
a. Hepburn Act.
b. Sixteenth Amendment.
c. Federal Reserve Act.
d. Clayton Antitrust Act.

20. Wilson's failure to support which one of the following issues during his first two years in office angered many progressives?
a. Reduced tariff duties on raw materials and manufactured goods.
b. Federal child labor reform.
c. Permanent federal regulation to check abuses of big business.
d. A reconstruction of the nation's banking and currency systems.

Completion: Insert the correct word or phrase to complete the following statements:

1. The belief that any effort to improve social conditions would prove fruitless because society is like a jungle in which only the "fittest" survive is embodied in the theory of

_____.

2. The founder in 1899 of one of the first settlement houses, Hull House in Chicago, was

_____.

3. The ban on the production, sale, and consumption of liquor achieved through the Eighteenth Amendment was called _____.

4. The author of the 1890 landmark book, *How the Other Half Lives*, was

_____.

5. The process of removing an official from office by popular vote is called a

_____.

6. Coined by Theodore Roosevelt, _____ was the journalistic practice of exposing economic, social, and political evils.

7. The popular name for the members of the Industrial Workers of the World was the

_____.

8. Organized in 1905 by African Americans, the _____ promoted racial integration, civil and political rights, and equal access to economic opportunity.

9. Woodrow Wilson's 1912 program that emphasized restoring conditions of free competition and equality of economic opportunity was called _____.

10. The government agency established in 1914 to provide regulatory oversight of business activity was the _____.

True/False: Indicate whether the following statements are true or false.

1. The "white slave traffic" referred to the exploitation of European immigrant labor in American industry. (T/F)

2. By 1914, more than fifty percent of the industrial labor force of the United States was foreign-born. (T/F)

3. Most AFL unions of the early twentieth century were inclusive encouraging the membership of women and African Americans. (T/F)

4. Theodore Roosevelt became, in 1901, the youngest man to ever hold the office of president of the United States. (T/F)

5. The Sixteenth Amendment to the United States Constitution repealed the federal income tax. (T/F)

Map Questions: Refer to the maps and accompanying information presented in the chapter to answer the following questions.

1. Chart Exercise: Review the statistical information presented in Immigration to the United States (1901-1920) and respond to the following questions: Identify the top three countries from which most immigrants to the United States came in the years between 1900 and 1920. Which three countries produced the least number of immigrants? How did patterns of immigration in the twentieth century differ from those of the nineteenth century? (page 572)

2. Label the states that went to Roosevelt in the Election of 1912. What was significant about Woodrow Wilson's victory as a Democrat? What caused the split in the Republican Party? What was significant about Eugene V. Deb's candidacy? (Map 21-1)

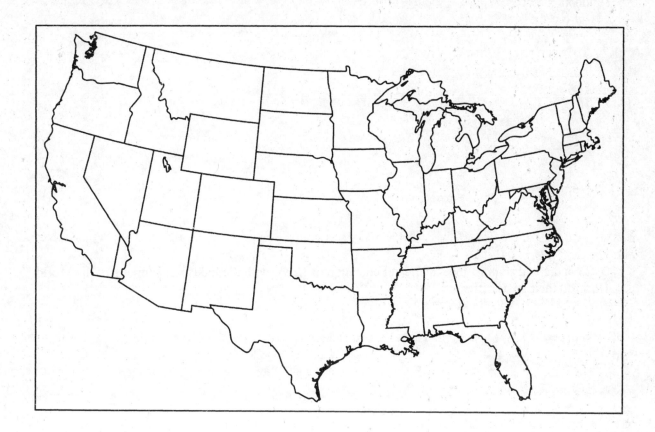

Short Answer Essay

1. What was the significance of the Henry House settlement and how effective was it in helping the residents it served?

2. Compare and contrast the American Federation of Labor with the Industrial Workers of the World. How did their goals differ?

3. Discuss the phrase "birth control." Why was it such a controversial issue at the turn of the twentieth century?

Extended Essay

1. Choose one key figure from each category on the Currents of Progressivism overview located on page 565. Identify the issues addressed by that individual as well as the established institutions or other achievements that resulted from their work. Discuss how these individuals, in particular, reflected the three basic attitudes associated with the Progressive movement in America.

2. Address the experiences of women, immigrants, and African Americans during the Progressive Era. What types of social and political developments affected their lives? What gains, if any, were made by members of these three groups throughout this period?

ANSWER KEY

Multiple Choice
1. d (562)
2. a (563)
3. c (564-565)
4. b (565)
5. d (567)
6. a (567)
7. c (567-568)
8. c (579)
9. b (569)
10. a (572)
11. d (573)
12. c (573)
13. a (575)
14. b (576)
15. c (577)
16. c (578-579)
17. d (580)
18. b (581)
19. a (581)
20. b (581)

Completion
1. Social Darwinism (563)
2. Jane Addams (564)
3. prohibition (566)
4. Jacob Riis (567)
5. recall (567)
6. muckraking (567)
7. Wobblies (575)
8. Niagara Movement (577)
9. New Freedom (580)
10. Federal Trade Commission (581)

True/False
1. F (569)
2. T (571)
3. F (574)
4. T (578)
5. F (581)

LECTURE NOTES:

Multiple Choice: Choose the response that best completes the statement or answers the question.

1. The issue that prompted vigilante activity in Bisbee, Arizona, had to do with
a. IWW violence.　　　　　　c. management-labor conflict.
b. the Red Scare.　　　　　　d. the Great Migration.

2. Which one of the following groups was NOT included in the vigilantes that participated in the Bisbee deportation?
a. The Citizens' Protective League　　　c. The American Federation of Labor
b. The Workers Loyalty League　　　　d. Company officials and small businessmen

3. All of the following statements about Theodore Roosevelt are true EXCEPT
a. He mediated the peace settlement of the Russo-Japanese War in 1905.
b. He invoked a corollary to the Monroe Doctrine to justify U.S. intervention in Latin America.
c. He authored the Fourteen Points.
d. He sent battleships to Japan to reinforce America's naval power in the Pacific.

4. Which of the following concepts were NOT, in Woodrow Wilson's opinion, hallmarks of American exceptionalism and the wave of the future?
a. Militarism and imperialism　　c. Democracy
b. Capitalism　　　　　　　　　d. Free trade

5. By 1916, United States policy in World War I can be best described as
a. neutral in name only.　　　　c. militarily prepared.
b. totally impartial.　　　　　　d. apathetic.

6. Which one of the following was NOT one of the events between February and March 1917 that prompted the United States to declare war on Germany?
a. Germany resumes unrestricted submarine warfare.
b. The Zimmerman note is intercepted and the contents revealed.
c. Germany sinks seven U.S. merchant ships.
d. German submarines sink the *Lusitania* and the Sussex.

7. The Committee on Public Information organized public support for the war effort by doing all of the following EXCEPT
a. producing pamphlets, articles, and books that explained the causes and meaning of the war.
b. enlisting the help of movie stars such as Charlie Chaplin to help sell war bonds.
c. conducting campaigns to reinforce the innocence and positive image of German-Americans.
d. raising a volunteer army of "Four Minute Men" to give brief patriotic speeches before stage shows and movies.

8. Which one of the following statements is NOT true of the African American experience in World War I?
a. African Americans were barred entirely from the United States Marines and Coast Guard.
b. African America soldiers were welcomed and organized into integrated units with white American soldiers.
c. Only about one in five African Americans actually saw combat.
d. African American soldiers of the 369th Infantry served with distinction in the French army and were awarded by the French government.

9. Which of the following statements about the United States military in World War I is NOT true?
a. Of the men who were called up to serve, 12 percent failed to report for duty.
b. Approximately 30,000 soldiers died from influenza and pneumonia while still in training camp.
c. Standardized tests given to soldiers showed illiteracy rates as low as 10 percent.
d. In the last seven weeks of fighting in France, U.S. soldiers used more ammunition than the entire Union army had in the Civil War.

10. The most important and long-lasting economic legacy of World War I for America was
a. a substantial increase in the federal debt.
b. the organizational shift toward corporatism in American business.
c. downturns in a number of industries.
d. an increase in overall farm production.

11. Which one of the following labor leaders was appointed by President Wilson to the National War Labor Board in 1918?
a. William "Big Bill" Haywood
b. Terrence Powderly
c. Samuel Gompers
d. Eugene V. Debs

12. World War I presented all of the following situations for women EXCEPT
a. a permanent presence in blue-collar jobs such as the defense industry where they earned the same wage as men.
b. a temporary opportunity to switch from low-paying jobs such as domestic service to higher-paying industrial employment.
c. a new awareness of women's work which resulted in the creation of the Women's Bureau in the Labor Department.
d. a unique opportunity to forge a national campaign for a constitutional amendment granting the vote to women.

13. Cases such as *Debs v. United States* and *Abrams v. United States* upheld
a. restrictions on union organizing during World War I.
b. the rights of labor to organize and strike.
c. government draft laws during World War I.
d. the constitutionality of the Espionage and Sedition Acts.

14. Which of the following statements about the Great Migration is NOT true?
a. In Northern cities, African Americans were free from the bigotry and racial violence they experienced in the South.
b. Kinship and community networks were crucial in spreading the news about job openings and housing in the North.
c. Single African American women often moved North before men because they could more easily obtain steady work.
d. Few African American men actually secured high-paying jobs in industry or manufacturing.

15. The biggest labor strike after World War I took place in which industry?
a. Railroads
b. Steel
c. Coal mining
d. Textiles

16. The "Big Four" was a reference to the
a. major points of Wilson's wartime peace plan.
b. locations of American victories in France.
c. "irreconcilables" who opposed the Versailles Treaty.
d. representatives of Great Britain, France, Italy, and the United States.

17. The most controversial of Wilson's Fourteen Points was
a. the creation of a League of Nations.　　c. national self-determination.
b. war-guilt for Germany.　　d. free trade.

18. Which one of the following was NOT a group in the United States Senate that opposed the ratification of the Versailles Treaty?
a. racist xenophobes　　c. labor supporters
b. Republican "irreconcilables"　　d. isolationist progressives

19. All of the following were consequences of the Red Scare EXCEPT
a. violations of constitutional rights.
b. government protection for trade unionism.
c. the deportation of hundreds of innocent people.
d. rising nativism and intolerance.

20. Which one of the following statements was NOT true of the election of 1920?
a. The Democratic Party was divided after the fight over the Treaty of Versailles.
b. The results showed the continued strength of progressivism.
c. Republicans won the election on the idea of a return to normalcy.
d. Americans wanted to stay out of international affairs.

Completion: Insert the correct word or phrase to complete the following statements:

1. The 1904 proclamation that justified for the United States to act as "an international police power" throughout Latin America was the _____.

2. At the onset of World War I, the allied nations of Great Britain, France, and Russia were known as the _____.

3. The government agency led by George Creel that sought to shape public opinion in support of the war was the _____.

4. The law establishing the military draft for World War I was the _____.

5. Although vague, the law which was used to crush criticism and dissent from groups like the Wobblies during World War I was the _____.

6. The _____ outlawed "any disloyal, profane, scurrilous, or abusive language intended to cause contempt, scorn, contumely, or disrepute" to the United States government, Constitution, or flag.

7. The mass movement of African Americans from the rural South to the urban North during World War I and the 1920s was termed the _____.

8. The international organization created after World War I to implement the principles of the Fourteen Points and resolve future international disputes was the _____.

9. The _____ formally ended World War I and created the League of Nations.

10. The post-World War I hysteria over Communist influence in the United States which was directed against labor activists and some ethnic groups was called the

_____.

True/False: Indicate whether the following statements are true or false.

1. Theodore Roosevelt was awarded the 1906 Nobel Peace Prize for mediating the settlement of the Russo-Japanese War at Portsmouth, New Hampshire, in 1905. (T/F)

2. During the Mexican Revolution, Great Britain, Japan, and the United States all formally recognized the regime of General Victoriano Huerta. (T/F)

3. More American soldiers died from influenza and pneumonia than in battle during World War I. (T/F)

4. The woman's right to vote was guaranteed through the ratification of the Eighteenth Amendment in 1919. (T/F)

5. As a result of the Great Migration, the black populations of Chicago and Detroit increased by 150 and 600 percent, respectively. (T/F)

Map Questions: Refer to the maps and accompanying information presented in the chapter to answer the following questions.

1. Identify the first state to award women the right to vote and the year in which it did so. Which eleven states did not guarantee women the right to vote until the Nineteenth Amendment was ratified in 1920? Which nine states never ratified the constitutional amendment and why not? (Map 22-2)

2. In what country did Americans see the most action in World War I? Where was the largest single American engagement of the war? Locate and label the locations of Allied victories from May through November, 1918. (Map 22-1)

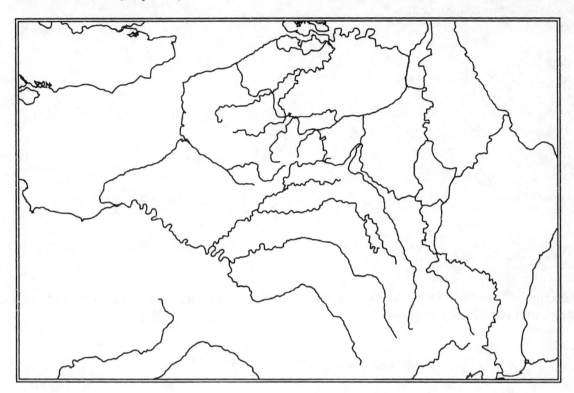

Short Answer Essay

1. In what ways did Woodrow Wilson attempt to guide the course of the Mexican Revolution and what were the consequences of these actions?

2. What led to the formation of the National Woman's Party and what strategies were used to achieve the passage of a woman suffrage amendment?

3. What were the three main elements of the Fourteen Points? Which was the most controversial of these elements and why?

Extended Essay

1. Trace the event leading to United States' involvement in World War I, including the importance of American neutrality, the sinking of the *Lusitania*, and the Zimmerman note. How did American entry into the war change the tide of the war and what impact did it have on America's economy, politics, and cultural life?

2. Address the experiences of African Americans, both enlisted and on the home front, during World War I. Describe the conditions that spurred the Great Migration from the rural South to the urban North and the consequences of this transition. Address as well the experiences of African American soldiers abroad and upon return home to the United States.

ANSWER KEY

Multiple Choice
1. c (588)
2. d (588)
3. c (589-590)
4. a (592)
5. a (593)
6. d (595)
7. c (595-596)
8. b (596)
9. c (596-598)
10. b (599-600)
11. c (600)
12. a (601)
13. d (604)
14. a (605)

15. b (606)
16. d (608)
17. a (607-608)
18. c (609)
19. b (610)
20. b (610)

Completion
1. Roosevelt Corollary (590)
2. Triple Entente (592)
3. Committee on Public Information (595)
4. Selective Service Act (596-597)
5. Espionage Act (600)

6. Sedition Act (604)
7. Great Migration (605)
8. League of Nations (607)
9. Treaty of Versailles (609)
10. Red Scare (610)

True/False
1. T (590)
2. F (591)
3. T (598)
4. F (603-604)
5. T (605-606)

Chapter Twenty-Three - The Twenties, 1920–1929

LECTURE NOTES:

Multiple Choice: Choose the response that best completes the statement or answers the question.

1. 1920s Hollywood represented for millions of Americans all of the following possibilities EXCEPT
a. material success.
c. the chance to remake one's identity.
b. upward mobility.
d. social authority.

2. Which one of the following statements about the "second industrial revolution" is NOT true?
a. Electricity replaced steam as the main power source for industry.
b. Newer, automatic machinery required a highly skilled labor force to operate.
c. Modern mass production techniques were applied to consumer goods such as automobiles and radios.
d. Industrial production in the 1920s nearly doubled.

3. The most successful corporations of the 1920s were those that led in all of the following key areas EXCEPT
a. corporate control and business leadership.
b. the integration of production and distribution.
c. product diversification.
d. the expansion of industrial research.

4. The control of a specific market by a few large producers is known as
a. monopoly.
c. welfare capitalism.
b. oligopoly.
d. the American plan.

5. Which of the following is NOT a direct consequence of the rise of the automobile industry in the 1920s?
a. A growth in urban and suburban development.
b. Increased markets for makers of steel, rubber, glass, and petroleum products.
c. New government standards for emissions and pollution control.
d. Transitions in leisure activities and courtship practices.

6. All of the following statements about farming in the 1920s are true EXCEPT
a. southern farming was still dominated by cotton production, causing the region to lag behind the rest of the nation in agricultural diversity and standard of living.
b. tenant farming decreased as agricultural laborers left for the cities.
c. net farm income and land values dropped compared to the war years.
d. American farmers suffered from a worldwide surplus of farm staples such as cotton, hogs, and corn.

7. The advertisers of the 1920s focused most of their attention on
a. the needs and desires of the consumer.
b. the quality of the product they were selling.
c. the price of the product.
d. pushing "American-Made" products.

8. Prior to the "radio mania" of the early 1920s, wireless technology was of primary interest to all of the following groups EXCEPT
a. advertising executives.
c. the military.
b. amateur operators.
d. the telephone industry.

9. The Teapot Dome scandal involved questionable federal involvement on the part of Interior Secretary Albert Fall in leasing
a. national forests to lumber companies.
b. navy oil reserves to oil developers.
c. buildings and supplies for the Veteran's Bureau.
d. federal facilities to violators of Prohibition statutes.

10. The three consecutive Republican presidents of the 1920s served in what order?
a. Hoover, Harding, Coolidge
b. Coolidge, Harding, Hoover
c. Harding, Hoover, Coolidge
d. Harding, Coolidge, Hoover

11. Secretary of the Treasury Andrew Mellon is most associated with
a. receiving bribes from violators of Prohibition statutes.
b. increasing American investment abroad.
c. advocating high tariff rates.
d. tax cuts for higher income brackets and businesses.

12. Herbert Hoover advocated all of the following ideals of business and commerce EXCEPT
a. the creation and expansion of national trade associations and regulatory commissions.
b. the creation of an "associative state" where government encouraged voluntary cooperation among corporations, consumers, workers, farmers, and small businessmen.
c. the standardization of key American industries which produced consumer products.
d. the preservation of American isolationism and a reduction in exports abroad.

13. The Eighteenth Amendment
a. repealed the Volstead Act.
b. gave an enormous boost to violent organized crime, which became a permanent feature of American life.
c. allowed a provision for those who produced alcoholic beverages for personal consumption only.
d. was easy to enforce once the Prohibition Bureau was established.

14. The "new immigrants" that entered the United States from 1890 to 1920 came primarily from
a. Mexico.   c. southern and eastern Europe.
b. Japan.   d. northern Europe.

15. The Ku Klux Klan of the 1920s targeted all of the following groups EXCEPT
a. Prohibitionists.   c. Jews.
b. Catholics.   d. African Americans.

16. Which of the following statements about the National Woman's Party is NOT true?
a. It was founded in 1916 by Alice Paul.
b. It largely represented the interests of business and professional women.
c. It focused on the passage of an Equal Rights Amendment to the Constitution, which was introduced to Congress in 1923.
d. It staunchly supported protective legislation for women.

17. All of the following statements about Mexican immigration in the 1920s are true EXCEPT
a. Mexicans were included in the immigration laws of 1921 and 1924.
b. Mexican immigration more than doubled in the 1920s compared to the previous decade.
c. Mexican immigrants often alternated between agricultural and factory jobs depending on the seasonal availability of work.
d. Mexican immigrants in the 1920s were likely to remain permanent residents of the United States.

18. African Americans such as Langston Hughes, Zora Neale Hurston, Paul Robeson, and others are most representative of the
a. opposition to Prohibition.
b. "New Negro" of the Harlem Renaissance.
c. Lost Generation.
d. Socialist Party.

19. Which one of the following groups would have been LEAST likely to vote for Al Smith in the 1928 election?
a. American Protective Association
c. "New" immigrants
b. Roman Catholics
d. Opponents of Prohibition

20. Which one of the following events is NOT correctly paired with the year in which it occurred?
a. The Scopes Trial/1925
b. KDKA goes on the air/1920
c. Charles Lindbergh makes first solo flight across the ocean/1927
d. F. Scott Fitzgerald publishes *The Great Gatsby*/1924

Completion: Insert the correct word or phrase to complete the following statements:

1. A paternalistic system of labor relations emphasizing management responsibility for employee well-being is called _____.

2. The 1929 community study by sociologists Robert and Helen Lynd which noted the dramatic impact of the car on social life was _____.

3. The affair involving Warren Harding's Interior Secretary, Albert Fall, who secretly leased navy oil reserves in exchange for cash, was the _____.

4. The 1920 law that defined forbidden liquor and established a federal Prohibition Bureau to enforce the Eighteenth Amendment was the _____.

5. Passed by Congress in 1921, the _____ set a maximum of 357,000 new immigrants into the United States each year.

6. Formed from the National American Woman Suffrage Association in 1921, the
_____ advocated the right for women to serve on juries and equal pay laws.

7. The first federal social welfare law passed in 1921 which provided federal funds for infant and maternity care was the _____.

8. A new African American cultural awareness that flourished in literature, art, and music in the 1920s was called the _____.

9. The first feature-length motion picture with sound produced by Warner Brothers in 1927 was
_____.

10. Created by Marcus Garvey, the _____ stressed black economic self-determination and unity among the black communities of the United States, the Caribbean, and Africa.

True/False: Indicate whether the following statements are true or false.

1. Herbert Hoover's presidential victory in 1928 was one of the largest popular and electoral landslides in the nation's history. (T/F)

2. Influential Pittsburgh banker Andrew Mellon served as secretary of the treasury under all three Republican presidents of the 1920s. (T/F)

3. The Ku Klux Klan of the 1920s staunchly opposed Prohibition and supported birth control and Darwinism. (T/F)

4. The Equal Rights Amendment (ERA) was supported by most women's groups and was passed by Congress in 1923. (T/F)

5. According to the U.S. Immigration Service, Mexican immigration to the United States in the 1920s more than doubled from the previous decade. (T/F)

Map Questions: Refer to the maps and accompanying information presented in the chapter to answer the following questions.

1. Locate and label the northern cities that drew the greatest number of African Americans in the 1920s. Which states had the highest percentage of African Americans? Which states had a population of over 50,000 African Americans? (Map 23-1)

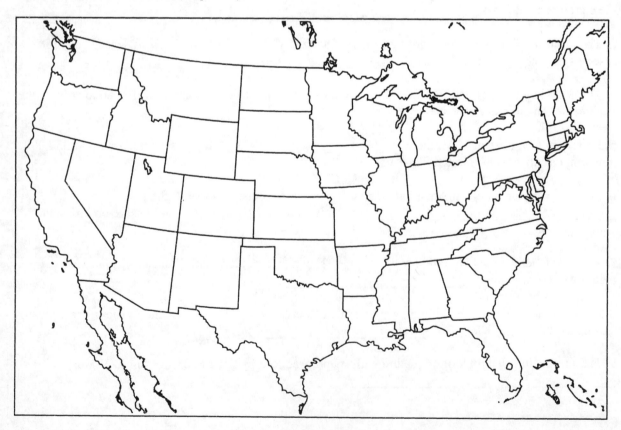

2. Label the states Democratic candidate Al Smith managed to carry in 1928. By what margin did Herbert Hoover win the election? What differences existed between Smith and Hoover that contributed to the outcome of the election? (Map 23-2)

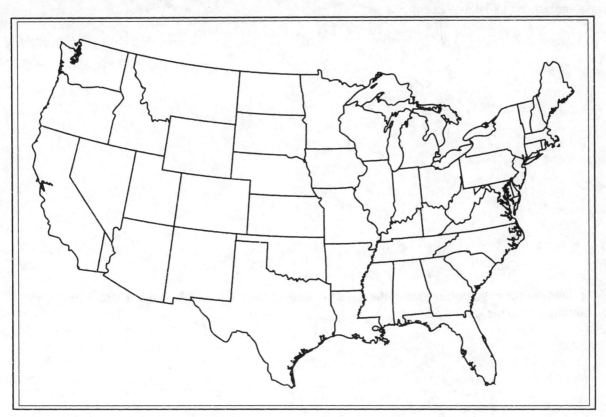

Short Answer Essay

1. Describe the "New Negro" of the Harlem Renaissance, identifying specific individuals and their contributions to the movement.

2. What explains the resurgence of the Ku Klux Klan in the 1920s and how did it affect the "new" immigrants to the United States?

3. How did the 1928 election and the candidates reflect the divisions in American society that emerged throughout the 1920s?

Extended Essay

1. Describe the structural changes in the American economy that developed in the 1920s and the effects those changes had on American life, including the shift from producer-durable goods to consumer-durable goods, the three key areas that brought success to modern corporations, as well as the impact that industries such as the automobile industry had on American society.

2. Describe the "New Woman" of the 1920s. How did women attempt to redefine their missions and reshape their strategies and what types of transitions took place in the women's movement during the era? How were women affected by the "new" morality of the age and how are these changes reflected in the advertisements presented on pages 640-642?

ANSWER KEY

Multiple Choice
1. d (616-617)
2. b (617)
3. a (617)
4. b (618)
5. c (620)
6. b (621)
7. a (622)
8. a (622)
9. b (625)
10. d (625-626)
11. d (625)
12. d (626)
13. b (627)
14. c (628)
15. a (629)
16. d (630)
17. a (631)
18. b (634)
19. a (635)
20. d (636)

Completion
1. welfare capitalism (618)
2. *Middletown* (619)
3. Teapot Dome (619)
4. Volstead Act (627)
5. Immigration Act (627)
6. League of Women Voters (630)
7. Sheppard-Towner Act (631)
8. Harlem Renaissance (634)
9. The Jazz Singer (623)
10. Universal Negro Improvement Association (634)

True/False
1. T (635)
2. T (625)
3. F (629)
4. F (630)
5. T (631)

LECTURE NOTES:

Multiple Choice: Choose the response that best completes the statement or answers the question.

1. The "Battle of the Running Bulls" referred to
a. problems associated with the bull market of the 1920s.
b. disagreements over government regulation of the cattle industry.
c. labor strife at General Motors in Flint, Michigan.
d. Roosevelt's conflict with Supreme Court justices.

2. Which one of the following was the most important weakness in the 1920s economy?
a. Too many Americans were invested in the stock market.
b. An extremely unequal distribution of income and wealth.
c. Consumers saved rather than spending their discretionary income.
d. Increasing mechanization encouraged overproduction by farmers.

3. Which one of the following statements is TRUE?
a. Unemployment during the depression never surpassed 20 percent.
b. Unemployment in 1939 was below 10 percent.
c. The unemployment crisis ended with Roosevelt's election.
d. Unemployment reached its peak in 1933.

4. The unemployment situation in the United States resulted in all of the following consequences EXCEPT
a. many workers blamed themselves for being unemployed.
b. women found it easier than men to hold onto their jobs.
c. unemployment compensation costs skyrocketed.
d. the psychological balance in the family changed.

5. Which of the following events did NOT occur in 1932?
a. Franklin D. Roosevelt inaugurated as 32nd President of the United States.
b. Farmer's Holiday Association organized in Iowa.
c. Bonus Army begins descending on Washington, D.C.
d. Four demonstrators are killed at the Ford River Rouge factory in Dearborn, Michigan.

6. When FDR became president, one of the first things he did to reestablish confidence in the economy was
a. set up the Temporary Emergency Relief Administration.
b. declare a four-day bank holiday to shore up the banking system.
c. establish the President's Emergency Committee for Unemployment.
d. have Congress create the Reconstruction Finance Corporation.

7. Which one of the following was NOT a measure that was passed during the first "Hundred Days"?
a. The Civilian Conservation Corps
b. The Federal Emergency Relief Administration
c. The Agricultural Adjustment Act
d. The Works Progress Administration

8. Which of the following individuals is NOT correctly paired with his/her program or accomplishment?
a. Frances Perkins/Secretary of Labor
b. Huey Long/Share Our Wealth
c. Robert F. Wagner/Congress of Industrial Organizations
d. Harold Ickes/Secretary of the Interior

9. All of the following individuals were critics of Roosevelt and the New Deal EXCEPT
a. Al Smith.
c. Harry Hopkins.
b. Huey Long.
d. Father Charles E. Coughlin.

10. Which of the following statements about the Congress of Industrial Organizations (CIO) is NOT true?
a. Membership in the organization was limited to skilled workers.
b. Many CIO organizers were Communists or radicals.
c. They called for the inclusion of black and women workers.
d. The CIO was formed by Sidney Hillman and John L. Lewis in 1935.

11. The "Dust Bowl" formed largely a consequence of
a. unprecedented periods of dry spells.
b. recurring tornadoes that touched down in the southern Great Plains.
c. excessive wheat farming which resulted in soil erosion and exposure of the topsoil to dust storms.
d. unusually frigid temperatures and blizzards in the region.

12. The Bureau of Reclamation of the Department of the Interior was responsible for all of the following projects in the late 1930s EXCEPT the
a. Boulder Dam.
c. All-American Canal.
b. Tennessee Valley Authority.
d. Grand Coulee Dam.

13. The 150-volume "Life in America" series, published as part of the Federal Writers Project, included all of the following EXCEPT
a. oral histories of former slaves.
c. pioneering collections of American songs and folk tales.
b. studies of ethnic and Indian cultures.
d. contemporary controversies and current events.

14. The Abraham Lincoln Brigade was
a. opposed to FDR's New Deal because it closely resembled Socialism.
b. a group of African American writers who collectively joined the Communist Party.
c. a voluntary American regiment, organized by the Communist Party, who fought in the Spanish Civil War against Franco.
d. a popular troop of vaudeville-type minstrel performers.

15. Which of the following statements about the Supreme Court in the 1930s is NOT true?
a. At FDR's request, Congress agreed to expand the Supreme Court from nine to a maximum of fifteen justices.
b. Its 1935 ruling in *Schecter v. United States* deemed the National Recovery Administration unconstitutional.
c. Its 1936 ruling in *Butler v. United States* invalidated the Agricultural Adjustment Administration.
d. The Court was composed mostly of Republican nominees, most of who were over age seventy.

16. Which of the following is least true of the impact of the Great Depression and New Deal for women?
a. New Deal agencies opened up spaces for scores of women in the federal bureaucracy.
b. The social work profession, which was two-thirds female, grew enormously in response to the relief and welfare programs.
c. A growing minority of women began working for wages and salaries outside the home.
d. Women developed an enormous and long-lasting level of political influence.

17. Eleanor Roosevelt is best described as a First Lady who
a. remained passive politically.
b. revolutionized the role of a political wife by turning the position into a base for independent action.
c. embraced her ceremonial role and engaged primarily in social activities.
d. appeared indifferent to the problems of the nation.

18. Which of the following statements about the New Deal's impact on minorities is TRUE?
a. The New Deal made explicit attempts to attack racism and discrimination in American life.
b. African American laborers filled a number of those jobs available through the TVA.
c. African Americans supported Roosevelt's New Deal, as evident by their new political allegiance to the Democratic Party.
d. Mexicans and Mexican Americans experienced better results from the New Deal than did African Americans.

19. While New Deal programs were less numerous by 1938, the Fair Standards Act established this for the first time:
a. federal minimum wage.   c. public housing construction.
b. credit card regulation.   d. environmental control standards.

20. The Wagner-Steagall Act of 1937
a. established the first federal minimum wage.
b. repealed Prohibition.
c. increased the number of Supreme Court Justices.
d. funded public housing construction.

Completion: Insert the correct word or phrase to complete the following statements:

1. The nation's worst economic crisis which produced bank failures, unemployment, and industrial and agricultural collapse is called the _____.

2. The _____ were unemployed veterans of World War I who descended upon Washington, D.C. in 1932 and demanded the cash bonuses promised by Congress in 1924.

3. FDR promised a "_____" for the American people, which became the title of the economic and political policies of his administration in the 1930s.

4. Speeches broadcast nationally over the radio in which FDR explained the steps he had taken to meet the financial emergency of the nation were called _____.

5. Passed by Congress in 1933, the _____ gave the president broad discretionary powers over all banking transactions and foreign exchange.

6. One of the most unique and controversial projects of the New Deal era was the _____, which, among other things, brought electricity for the first time to people in six Southern states.

7. The 1935 act which established federal old-age pensions and unemployment insurance was the _____.

8. The _____ was an alliance of industrial unions that spurred the 1930s organizational drive among the mass-production industries.

9. The _____ helped many notable American writers survive the Depression by employing over 5,000 of them on a variety of projects.

10. The 1935 Supreme Court case of *Schecter v. United States* found the
_____ unconstitutional in its entirety.

True/False: Indicate whether the following statements are true or false.

1. The single-leading cause of the Great Depression was the stock market crash of 1929. (T/F)

2. Herbert Hoover's plan for economic recovery was centered on restoring the confidence of the consumer and included large-scale humanitarian efforts. (T/F)

3. The "brains trust" modeled their economic reform after the old progressive dream of recreating an ideal society of small producers. (T/F)

4. The Resettlement Administration was successful in moving nearly 100% of the projected 500,000 destitute farm families. (T/F)

5. Communists were strong supporters of FDR's New Deal and were influential in a variety of WPA arts projects. (T/F)

Map Questions: Refer to the maps and accompanying information presented in the chapter to answer the following questions.

1. What ecological conditions caused the Dust Bowl? What states were affected by the Dust Bowl? Where was it most severe? What federal programs were created to respond to the problem and what effect did they have on the people of those regions? (Map 24-2)

2. Label the states Hoover managed to carry in 1932. How did FDR's popular vote compare to Hoover's in the election of 1928? Did the election of 1932 represent a rejection of Herbert Hoover, or an affirmation of Franklin D. Roosevelt? (Map 24-1)

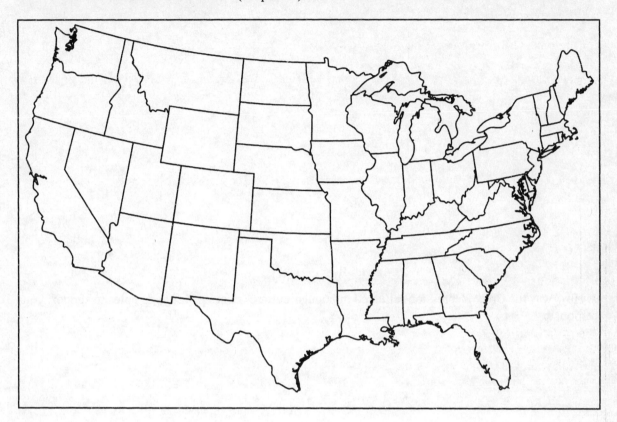

Short Answer Essay

1. Describe the Flint sit-down strike of 1936 and evaluate the significance of this strike.

2. How was the Great Depression reflected in popular culture? Use specific examples to support your response.

3. What was the impact of the New Deal on women and minorities?

Extended Essay

1. What were the underlying causes of the Great Depression? What type of psychological, social, and financial consequences did it have for most Americans? How did the Hoover administration respond to the Depression?

2. Describe FDR's New Deal. How did FDR attempt to restore economic confidence in the United States? How did the New Deal support the growth of organized labor? Who were the critics of the New Deal and what was the basis of their criticism?

ANSWER KEY

Multiple Choice
1. c (644)
2. b (646-647)
3. d (647)
4. c (647-648)
5. a (649-650)
6. b (651)
7. d (652)
8. c (653-655)
9. c (653-654)
10. a (656)
11. c (658)
12. b (659)
13. d (660)
14. c (662)
15. a (668)

16. d (663-664)
17. b (664)
18. c (665)
19. a (666)
20. d (666)

Completion
1. Great Depression (645)
2. Bonus Army (650)
3. New Deal (650)
4. fireside chats (651)
5. Emergency Banking Act (651)
6. Tennessee Valley Authority (653)
7. Social Security Act (654)

8. Congress of Industrial Organization (656)
9. Federal Writers Project (660)
10. National Recovery Administration (663)

True/False
1. F (645)
2. F (649)
3. F (651)
4. T (655)
5. T (662)

Chapter Twenty-Five - World War II, 1941–1945

LECTURE NOTES:

Multiple Choice: Choose the response that best completes the statement or answers the question.

1. The Los Alamos community was an example of a

a. Japanese American internment camp.

b. unique group of scientists conducting war research.

c. new military training base built in the West.

d. 1941 industrial labor strike.

2. Roosevelt set up the atomic bomb project because he feared this country might successfully develop an atomic bomb:

a. Japan.

b. the Soviet Union.

c. Nazi Germany.

d. Fascist Italy.

3. Hitler's invasion of this country prompted a joint declaration of war from Great Britain and France in September, 1939:

a. Austria

b. Ethiopia

c. Poland

d. France

4. Which one of the following was NOT an action the United States took before its formal entry into World War II?

a. Meeting with Britain to draw up Atlantic Charter principles.

b. A lend-lease policy to Britain and the Soviet Union.

c. U.S. ships to shoot on sight any Nazi ship in U.S. "defensive waters."

d. Asking the League to "quarantine the aggressors."

5. The first beneficiary of massive aid from the United States as a consequence of the Lend-Lease Act was

a. China.

b. Great Britain.

c. France.

d. the Soviet Union.

6. In addition to Pearl Harbor, Japan struck U.S. bases in all of the following locations on December 7, 1941 EXCEPT

a. Cuba.

b. Philippines.

c. Wake Island.

d. Guam.

7. Which of the following was NOT a power granted to the president under the War Powers Act?

a. Establish programs censoring all information and abridging civil liberties.

b. Seize foreign-owned property.

c. Reorganize the federal government and create new agencies.

d. Adjust the tax structure to pay for excessive wartime spending.

8. Defense production for World War II most dramatically affected the wage-earning patterns of this group:
a. women
b. Native Americans
c. African Americans
d. Mexicans

9. All of the following statements about American labor during World War II are true EXCEPT
a. Union membership for women increased from 11 to 23 percent.
b. The level of strike activity between 1941 and 1945 was greater than any other four-year period in history.
c. African American union membership decreased, due largely to "hate strikes" that forced them out of unions.
d. Major unions agreed to no-strike pledges for the duration of the war.

10. Signed by President Roosevelt on February 19, 1942, Executive Order 9066
a. froze the financial assets of the Issei.
b. barred Japanese immigrants from U.S. citizenship.
c. authorized a program for gradual release of interned Japanese-Americans.
d. suspended the civil rights and authorized the exclusion of more than 100,000 Japanese Americans from designated military areas.

11. The focus of activity by the NAACP in the 1940s was
a. discrimination in the military.
b. equal employment opportunities.
c. fair housing.
d. segregation in public facilities.

12. The zoot-suit riots involved uniformed sailors assaulting youth from this community:
a. African American.
b. Japanese American.
c. Mexican American.
d. Italian American.

13. Before the outbreak of World War II in 1939, the majority of men in the U.S. armed forces were
a. in the National Guard.
b. employed as military police.
c. Army reservists.
d. poised and ready to fight.

14. Which of the following individuals is not correctly matched with his respective position during World War II?
a. Henry Stimson/Secretary of War
b. General Douglas MacArthur/Supreme Commander in the Pacific
c. General George Marshall/Army Chief of Staff
d. General Dwight D. Eisenhower/Commander, Joint Chiefs of Staff

15. Women served during World War II in all of the following capacities EXCEPT the
a. Naval Special Warfare combat forces.
b. Army Nurse Corps.
c. Women's Airforce Service Pilots.
d. Marine Corps Women's Reserve.

16. Operation Overlord involved the D-Day invasion of
a. Sicily.
b. Normandy.
c. North Africa.
d. the Philippines.

17. The Japanese offensive threat to Hawaii and the west coast of the United States was ended at the
a. Battle of the Bulge.
b. Battle of the Coral Sea.
c. Battle of Midway.
d. Battle of Guadalcanal.

18. Which one of the following individuals was not one of the "Big Three" who met at the Yalta Conference in February 1945?
a. Franklin D. Roosevelt
b. Harry S Truman
c. Josef Stalin
d. Winston Churchill

19. Roosevelt and his advisers followed this policy in relation to Holocaust death camps:
a. It was propaganda, similar to World War I fabrications.
b. Total Allied victory was the best way to liberate the camps.
c. Civilian rescues would be employed to distract the enemy.
d. Soviet troops were closer and, therefore, should liberate the camps.

20. While lower than other allies, the human cost of World War II for Americans was second only to
a. the American Revolution.
b. the Vietnam War.
c. World War I.
d. the Civil War.

Completion: Insert the correct word or phrase to complete the following statements:

1. FDR's position of providing "all aid to the allies short of war" was clarified in the _____, which permitted the sale of arms to Britain, France, and China.

2. The opponents of the United States and its allies in World War II were called the _____.

3. Passed by Congress in March 1941, the _____ arranged for the transfer of war supplies to those nations whose defense was considered vital to the defense of the United States in World War II.

4. The August 1941 agreement between Franklin Roosevelt and British Prime Minister Winston Churchill which specified the right of all peoples to live in freedom from fear, want, and tyranny was called the _____.

5. Passed by Congress in December 1941, the _____ gave the president the power to reorganize the federal government and create new wartime agencies.

6. The image of _____ appeared in posters and advertisements to draw women into the workplace for the duration of World War II.

7. Formed by pacifists in 1942, the _____ was just one of the civil rights organizations that were formed during wartime to fight discrimination at home and in the U.S. armed forces.

8. United States citizens born of immigrant Japanese parents, members of the _____ fought heroically in Italy and France and became the most decorated regiment in World War II.

9. United States and British invasion of France in June 1944 during World War II was called _____.

10. The final stages of the war and postwar arrangements were planned during the February 1945 final meeting of Roosevelt, Churchill, and Stalin, held at _____.

True/False: Indicate whether the following statements are true or false.

1. On December 8, 1941, Roosevelt asked Congress for a declaration of war against Japan and its European allies, Germany and Italy. (T/F)

2. Due to the costliness of the war, the federal government spent twice as much during World War II as during its entire prior history. (T/F)

3. More workers went on strike in 1941 in the United States than in any previous year except 1919. (T/F)

4. Executive Order 8802 suspended the civil rights of Japanese Americans and authorized the exclusion of more than 112,000 men, women, and children. (T/F)

5. More than 1,000 enlisted members of the Women's Airforce Service Pilots flew planes during combat missions in Africa, Italy, and France. (T/F)

Map Questions: Refer to the maps and accompanying information presented in the chapter to answer the following questions.

1. Who were the Allied Powers? Who were the Axis Powers? Where were the locations of major battles and Allied victories? What were the key turning points of the war in Europe? (Map 25-1)

2. Illustrate the extent of Japanese control in the Pacific by August 1942. Label the locations of Japanese victories. Label the locations of Allied victories. On which cities and on what dates were the atomic bombs dropped? (Map 25-2)

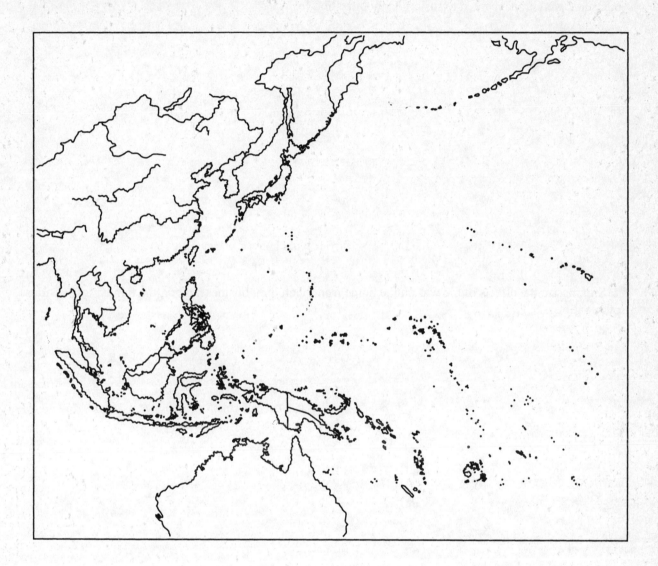

Short Answer Essay

1. Describe how Roosevelt set out to make the United States a "great arsenal of democracy." What measures were implemented to foster the mobilization for war?

2. Summarize the effects of the war on the home front, including business, labor, the family, and various ethnic groups.

3. Address the issue of Japanese internment. How were the civil rights of Japanese Americans violated during World War II?

Extended Essay

1. Trace the involvement of the United States in World War II, including those events that foreshadowed the outbreak of war in Europe and the Pacific. What advantages did the Allies have that allowed for a victory in Europe and the Pacific? What were the significant turning points of the war and changes that developed in the last stages of the war?

2. Use of the atomic bomb in World War II presents one of the most controversial aspects of the war and is often a topic of debate. Trace the development of the bomb, from the work at Los Alamos to Truman's decision to drop the bomb in the final stages of the war. What were the consequences of this action, both short-term and long-term?

ANSWER KEY

Multiple Choice
1. b (672)
2. c (672)
3. c (674)
4. d (675)
5. b (675)
6. a (676)
7. d (677)
8. a (679)
9. c (680)
10. d (681-683)
11. a (683)
12. c (684)
13. b (685)
14. d (686-687)
15. a (686-689)
16. b (693)
17. c (694)
18. b (698)
19. b (697)
20. d (699)

Completion
1. Neutrality Act of 1939 (675)
2. Axis Powers (675)
3. Lend-Lease Act (675)
4. Atlantic Charter (675)
5. War Power Act (677)
6. Rosie the Riveter (679)
7. Congress of Racial Equality (683)
8. 442nd (687)
9. Operation Overlord (693)
10. Yalta (698)

True/False
1. F (676)
2. T (678)
3. T (680)
4. F (682)
5. F (686)

Chapter Twenty-Six - The Cold War, 1945–1952

LECTURE NOTES:

Multiple Choice: Choose the response that best completes the statement or answers the question.

1. The main effect of the Red Scare on college campuses in America was the
a. restraint of free speech.   c. increasing radicalism of students.
b. sharp decline in enrollment.   d. increase in racism and discrimination.

2. Which of the following is NOT a consequence of the creation of the World Bank and International Monetary fund?
a. Stabilized exchange rates to permit the expansion of international trade.
b. The United States became principal supplier of funds, donating more than $7 billion to each organization.
c. The possibility of providing aid to people of the Soviet Union and its Eastern European client states was realized by the USSR's participation in the conference.
d. The world economy could be unilaterally shaped by the United States, who determined the allocation of loans.

3. Which one of the following statements is NOT true of the United Nations?
a. Only five nations, excluding the Soviet Union, served permanently on the Security Council.
b. Each nation represented on the Security Council enjoyed absolute veto power over the decisions of the other members.
c. One of the first delegates to the United Nations from the United States was Eleanor Roosevelt.
d. The United Nations achieved its greatest success with humanitarian programs.

4. The Truman Doctrine was first applied to these countries:
a. North and South Korea.   c. Turkey and Greece.
b. East and West Berlin.   d. Yugoslavia and Alabania.

5. The 8000-word "long telegram," which largely established the U.S. foreign policy of "containment" towards the Soviet Union, was authored by
a. George C. Marshall.   c. Winston Churchill.
b. George F. Kennan.   d. Harry Truman.

6. The Marshall Plan was aimed at doing all of the following EXCEPT
a. turning back socialist and Communist electoral bids for power in northern and Western Europe.
b. rebuilding and integrating Germany into a unified region compatible with U.S. political and economic interests.
c. bringing all recipients of aid into a bilateral agreement with the United States.
d. reducing commercial barriers among member nations and opening all to U.S. trade and investment.

7. Which one of the following organizations created the mechanisms for military enforcement through a mutual defense policy between the United States and Western European nations?
a. GATT   c. NATO
b. U.S. Department of Defense d. The Warsaw Pact

8. The Council of Economic Advisors to the president was created as a result of the
a. Taft-Hartley Act.   c. Smith-Mundt Act.
b. Employment Act of 1946.   d. McCarran Act.

9. Which one of the following former "New Dealers" posed a bid for the presidency against Truman in the 1948 election?
a. Henry Wallace   c. Harold Ickes
b. Harry Hopkins   d. Eleanor Roosevelt

10. Which one of the following actions did NOT help Truman win the election of 1948?
a. Desegregating the armed forces.
b. Recognition for the new state of Israel.
c. The success of the Berlin airlift.
d. Painting Wallace as a tool of the communists.

11. The National Security Act of 1947 established all of the following agencies EXCEPT the
a. Department of Defense.
b. National Security Council.
c. National Security Resources Board.
d. Federal Bureau of Investigation.

12. Measures included in the Federal Employees Loyalty and Security Program and the McCarran Act reflected an inherent prejudice specifically aimed towards this group:
a. women.
c. homosexuals.
b. African Americans.
d. Mexican immigrants.

13. Which one of the following was called by President Truman "the greatest danger to freedom of the press, speech, and assembly since the Sedition Act of 1798?"
a. The National Security Act of 1947
b. The Federal Employees Loyalty and Security Program
c. The Internal Security Act
d. The Immigration and Nationality Act

14. Joseph McCarthy's red-hunting tactics finally backfired when he attempted to expose Communists in the ranks of this organization:
a. The U.S. State Department.
c. The Civil Rights Congress.
b. The U.S. army.
d. The Democratic Party.

15. All of the following statements about post-war American women are true EXCEPT:
a. Women represented more than 50% of all college graduates by 1950.
b. Women were encouraged by experts to devote themselves full-time to homemaking and child rearing.
c. Many women worked primarily to maintain the new middle-class standard of living.
d. Most women who continued to work after World War II did so in minimum-wage jobs in the service sector.

16. Which one of the followings states had the highest proportion of its state income from federal military dollars during the Cold War?
a. New Mexico
c. Utah
b. Texas
d. California

17. The 1947 federal "Zeal for Democracy" program promoted strengthening national security and fighting Soviet communism through
a. public education.
c. religion.
b. the family.
d. the Freedom Train.

18. The Korean War began when
a. Communist China invaded Korea to keep Nationalist China out.
b. the Soviet Union joined its North Korean ally in an invasion.
c. North Korea launched a military attack on South Korea.
d. South Korea attempted to unify both occupation zones of Korea.

19. Truman derived his authority to commit the United States to war in Korea from
a. a Congressional declaration of war.
b. the NATO charter.
c. National Security Council Paper 68.
d. a recommendation from the Joint Chiefs of Staff.

20. All of the following were consequences of the Korean War EXCEPT
a. A quadrupled U.S. defense budget.
b. A strengthened case for rolling back communism.
c. The expansion of anti-Communist propaganda.
d. The loss of 54,000 American lives and more than 2 million North Korean and Chinese.

Completion: Insert the correct word or phrase to complete the following statements:

1. The policy announced in 1947 that laid down the first plank in a global campaign against communism was the _____.

2. The European Recovery Plan of June 5, 1947, which committed the United States to help in the rebuilding of post-World War II Europe was introduced by _____.

3. Formed in 1949, the _____ involved a mutual defense pact between the United States and ten European nations.

4. The 1947 _____ substantially limited the tools available to labor unions in labor-management disputes.

5. Passed by Congress in July 1947, the Department of Defense and the _____ were established to coordinate defense policies and advise the president.

6. Made a permanent standing committee in 1945, the _____ was charged with investigating "un-American" propaganda that attacked constitutional government.

7. The Wisconsin Senator whose name provided the label for the entire campaign to silence critics of the Cold War was _____.

8. 1944 legislation that eased the return of veterans into American society by providing educational and employment benefits was the _____.

9. The 1950 policy statement that committed the United States to a military approach to the Cold War was _____.

10. Launched by the federal Office of Education in 1947, the _____ program was charged with promoting and strengthening democratic thinking and practice in schools.

True/False: Indicate whether the following statements are true or false.

1. The "iron curtain" reference was coined by President Harry Truman in a 1946 speech delivered in Fulton, Missouri. (T/F)

2. Executive order 9835, signed on March 21, 1947, desegregated the armed forces and banned discrimination in the federal civil service. (T/F)

3. Adopted in 1952, the Immigration and Nationality Act barred people deemed "subversive" or "homosexual" from becoming citizens or visiting the United States. (T/F)

4. By 1952, two million more wives worked outside the home than did during World War II. (T/F)

5. Truman's decision to institute a peacetime draft in 1948 and order American troops into Korea was sanctioned by a formal declaration of war from the United States Congress. (T/F)

Map Questions: Refer to the maps and accompanying information presented in the chapter to answer the following questions.

1. What political parties (and their respective candidates) were represented in the election of 1948? What were Truman's strengths/weaknesses? What were Dewey's? What led to the candidacy of Strom Thurmond? (Map 26-2)

2. Locate and label the countries included in NATO. Locate and label the countries included in the
Warsaw Pact. How was Germany divided and occupied? (Map 26-1)

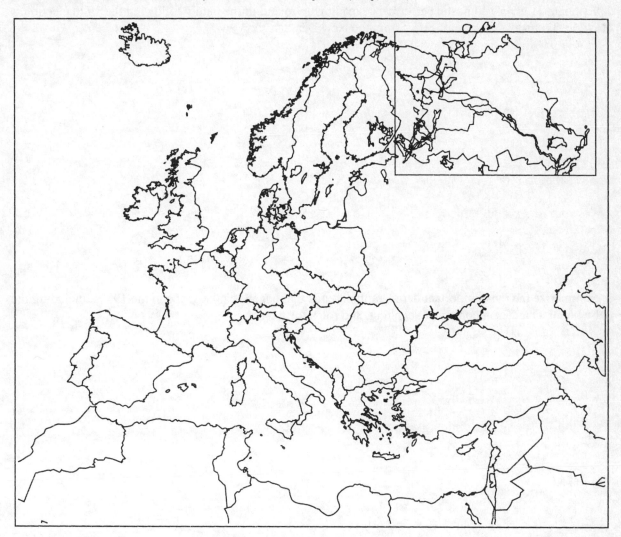

Short Answer Essay

1. Evaluate Truman's domestic performance leading up to and immediately following the 1948 election. How did Truman's "Fair Deal" differ from the New Deal?

2. Summarize the most important demographic trends that began to take shape in the 1950s, including the baby boom, changes in consumer spending, and roles for women.

3. What contributed to the rise of McCarthyism? Discuss the major causes, personalities, and events of the Red Scare.

Extended Essay

1. Trace the development of the military and economic policies that shaped the postwar world, outlining America's involvement in the creation of these policies. What steps were taken to promote growth in the postwar global economy? How did American foreign policy respond to the mounting situations in Europe?

2. Discuss the role of the United States in Korea in the decade after World War II. Why did Truman feel compelled to act in South Korea? What was China's role in Korea? How did the war effect the 1952 election and why did Eisenhower win the election?

ANSWER KEY

Multiple Choice
1. a (707)
2. c (707-708)
3. a (709)
4. c (710)
5. b (710)
6. d (710)
7. c (712-713)
8. b (714)
9. a (718)
10. a (715)
11. d (717)
12. c (718)
13. c (718)
14. b (720-721)

15. a (723)
16. d (723-724)
17. a (725)
18. c (727)
19. c (728)
20. b (729)

Completion
1. Truman Doctrine (709)
2. George C. Marshall (710)
3. North Atlantic Treaty Organization - NATO (712)
4. Taft-Hartley Act (715)
5. National Security Council (717)

6. HUAC (719)
7. Joseph McCarthy (720)
8. GI Bill (723)
9. National Security Council Paper 68 (728)
10. Zeal for Democracy (725)

True/False
1. F (709)
2. F (718)
3. T (718)
4. T (722)
5. F (728)

Chapter Twenty-Seven - America at Midcentury, 1952–1963

LECTURE NOTES:

Multiple Choice: Choose the response that best completes the statement or answers the question.

1. Which of the following is NOT true of rock 'n' roll music?
a. It reflected a cultural integration that was later realized socially and politically during the Civil Rights Movement.
b. It demonstrated the enormous consumer power of American teenagers.
c. Institutional racism did not exist at all in the music industry.
d. American teenagers found a new sense of community through music.

2. All of the following occurred during Eisenhower's presidency EXCEPT
a. The Department of Health, Education, and Welfare was created.
b. The Submerged Lands Act was passed.
c. Federal spending on agriculture increased.
d. The Social Security system was dismantled.

3. The National Defense Education Act was a bipartisan effort led by Eisenhower in response to the Soviet
a. development of the hydrogen bomb.
b. launching the Sputnik satellite.
c. announcement of a manned space flight.
d. U-2 spy flights.

4. Which of the following did NOT characterize suburban life in the 1950s?
a. Attainable by only educated, middle-class professionals.
b. The nuclear family as the model for American life.
c. Architectural and psychological conformity.
d. Distinctive neighborhood identities resulting from self-segregation and zoning ordinances.

5. In 1955, the newly combined AFL-CIO
a. included only one in eight nonagricultural members.
b. reached its apex of membership.
c. was closely tied to organized crime.
d. made a commitment to bring unorganized workers into the fold.

6. Public recognition of teenagers' special status during the 1950s was reinforced by all of the following EXCEPT
a. a separate legal designation defined by the Supreme Court.
b. the increasing uniformity of public school education.
c. experts who published guidebooks and manuals for parents.
d. the marketplace and media.

7. Which one of the following statements is NOT true?
a. Juvenile crime in the 1950s increased.
b. The dollar value of annual record sales nearly tripled between 1954 and 1959.
c. The most common age at which American females married in the late 50s was twenty.
d. 1950s rock 'n' roll music gave rise to deep anxieties about more open expression of sexual feelings.

8. Television shows like *Father Knows Best* and *Leave It to Beaver*
a. featured working-class, urban ethnic families.
b. epitomized the ideal non-ethnic, white suburban American family.
c. addressed difficult social issues of the day.
d. incorporated African-American families into a number of plots.

9. Political advertisements for presidential candidates were first seen on television in
a. 1956.
b. 1960.
c. 1950.
d. 1952.

10. The 1957 novel *On the Road*
a. chronicled events along the campaign trail during the 1956 election.
b. became the "manifesto" of the Beat generation.
c. severely altered political life in the 1950s.
d. celebrated the American virtues of progress, power, and material gain.

11. Eisenhower's Secretary of State, John Foster Dulles, called for a "new look" in American foreign policy that
a. increased heavy-handed interventionist diplomacy in Latin America.
b. called for a greater reliance of America's nuclear superiority.
c. denounced the "spy wars" and covert action of the Truman administration.
d. totally voided the containment policy of Truman and Kennan.

12. One of the first psychological "thaws" in the Cold War came in 1959 when
a. Khrushchev made a twelve-day trip to America.
b. Khrushchev publicly condemned Stalin's crimes.
c. Eisenhower formally apologized to Khrushchev for entering Soviet airspace.
d. Eisenhower agreed to end all spy flights.

13. Eisenhower's position on Cold War defense spending and missile development is best described as
a. liberal.
b. conservative.
c. moderate.
d. indifferent.

14. The most publicized CIA intervention of the Eisenhower years took place in
a. 1953 in Iran.
b. 1954 in Vietnam.
c. 1950 in Korea.
d. 1954 in Guatemala.

15. Eisenhower used the domino theory to justify America's intervention in
a. Vietnam.
b. Iran.
c. Guatemala.
d. Korea.

16. Which of the following statements pertaining to Eisenhower's warning about the "military industrial complex" in NOT true?
a. Eisenhower outlined the dangers of it in his farewell address in January 1961.
b. The concept emerged as a result of Eisenhower's own fears and doubts about the arms race.
c. Eisenhower reinforced his support for the union of a large military establishment and a large arms industry as necessary to the democratic process.
d. Eisenhower cautioned that the combination had "the potential for the disastrous rise of misplaced power."

17. All of the following statements about John F. Kennedy are true EXCEPT

a. his political career began in the Massachusetts House of Representatives in 1946.

b. he resembled Dwight Eisenhower both in personality and temperament.

c. he won the Pulitzer Prize in 1957 for his book Profiles in Courage.

d. he defeated Lyndon B. Johnson for the Democratic nomination in 1960.

18. Which one of the following was NOT introduced as part of Kennedy's New Frontier?

a. The Peace Corps

b. The Equal Pay Act

c. The Social Security Act

d. The National Aeronautics and Space Administration

19. The 1961 Bay of Pigs "debacle" most reflected

a. the limitations of presumptuous Cold War attitudes possessed by the CIA and the United States government.

b. the ability of the CIA to incite an uprising in an attempt to remove an unpopular dictator.

c. the efficiency of U.S. military forces in leading an invasion.

d. an end of CIA support for anti-Castro operations.

20. When Khrushchev agreed to withdraw missiles from Cuba, Kennedy agreed to

a. withdraw missiles from West Germany.

b. increase communications between the U.S. and the U.S.S.R.

c. sign a limited nuclear test-ban agreement.

d. respect Cuban sovereignty and not invade the island.

Completion: Insert the correct word or phrase to complete the following statements:

1. The 1956 measure that provided federal funding to build a nationwide system of interstate and defense highways was called the _____.

2. The _____ called for reunification and national elections in Vietnam in 1956.

3. The area located on Cuba's south coast known as the _____ was the site of an unsuccessful landing by fourteen hundred anti-Castro Cuban Refugees in April 1961.

4. The most serious confrontation of the Cold War, _____, in October 1962 was brought about by the placement of Soviet nuclear missiles in Cuba.

5. Creating a _____ was the theme of the Johnson administration in regards to the continued focus on domestic issues such as poverty, education, and civil rights.

6. The 1959 act that widened government control over union affairs known as the _____ further restricted union use of picketing and secondary boycotts during strikes.

7. The precursor to Johnson's Great Society was John F. Kennedy's _____, the domestic and foreign policy initiatives designed to reinvigorate a sense of national purpose and energy.

8. The _____ was the federal agency created in 1958 to manage American space flights and exploration.

9. The Kennedy administration's 10 year, $100 billion plan to spur economic development in Latin America known as the _____ was unveiled in 1961.

10. The _____ signed in August 1963 by the United States, Britain, and the Soviet Union outlawed nuclear testing in the atmosphere, in outer space, and under water.

True/False: Indicate whether the following statements are true or false.

1. Prior to Dwight D. Eisenhower's election, Ulysses S. Grant was the last two-term Republican president. (T/F)

2. The single largest public works program in American history was the Federal Highway Act of 1956. (T/F)

3. As a former WWII Commander, President Dwight D. Eisenhower realized the importance of exploring space; as a result, the U.S. launched the first space-orbiting satellite in history in October, 1952. (T/F)

4. The Equal Pay Act of 1963 helped revive the issue of women's rights and was led by First Lady Jackie Kennedy. (T/F)

5. The Bay of Pigs was the most serious confrontation of the Cold War. (T/F)

Map Questions: Refer to the maps and accompanying information presented in the chapter to answer the following questions.

1. What factors contributed to the 1960 election being one of the closest in American history? Where did each candidate run the strongest? How did the popular vote for each candidate compare to the electoral vote? (Map 27-2)

2. Besides Florida, identify from this map the United States' possessions. Where are U.S. military bases located? In which area did overt military actions occur? Identify which nations gained independence and the respective dates. (Map 27-1)

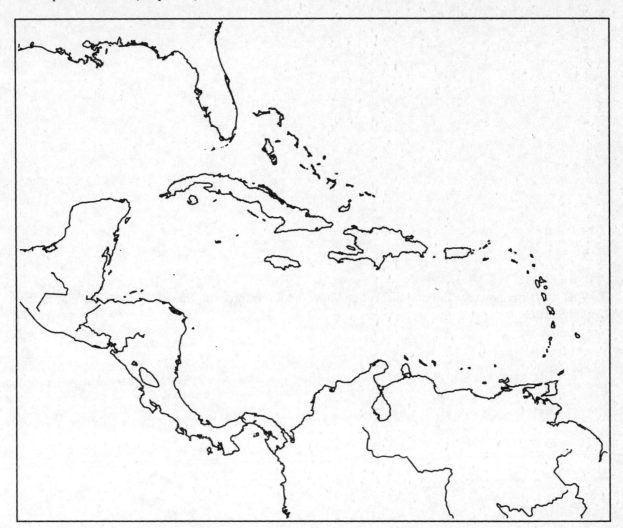

Short Answer Essay

1. Describe the music in Memphis that influenced Elvis Presley and how he contributed to the development of rock 'n' roll.

2. What was Eisenhower's "domino theory" and how did it reinforce the "mood" of the Cold War in the United States?

3. How did Kennedy's election change the direction of the nation? Discuss the successes and failures of Kennedy's New Frontier.

Extended Essay

1. Discuss the basic elements of "mass culture" during the 1950s and the reasons behind the expansion of the youth market. What role did television play in politics, as well as in projecting images of American society during this period? What place did teens hold in the postwar affluence? Who were the critics of these trends and what was the basis of their criticisms?

2. Describe United States foreign policy during the period of 1952-1963. What prompted United States intervention in Central America and Southeast Asia? Detail the events surrounding the Bay of Pigs and the Cuban Missile Crisis. Based on these events, do you think Eisenhower's warning about the "military industrial complex" was justified? Why or why not?

ANSWER KEY

Multiple Choice
1. c (738-739)
2. d (739)
3. b (741)
4. a (741-742)
5. b (742-743)
6. a (743-744)
7. c (745)
8. b (746)
9. d (746)
10. b (746-747)
11. b (747)
12. a (747)
13. c (747)
14. d (748)
15. a (750)
16. c (750)
17. b (750-751)
18. c (752)
19. a (753-754)
20. d (754)

Completion
1. Federal Highway Act (741)
2. Geneva Accord (750)
3. Bay of Pigs (754)
4. Cuban Missile Crisis (754)
5. Great Society (755)
6. Landrum-Griffin Act (743)
7. New Frontier (751)
8. National Aeronautics and Space Administration (NASA) (752)
9. Alliance for Progress (753)
10. Limited Nuclear Test-Ban Treaty (754)

True/False
1. T (739)
2. T (741)
3. F (747)
4. F (751)
5. F (754)

Chapter Twenty-Eight - The Civil Rights Movement, 1945–1966

LECTURE NOTES:

Multiple Choice: Choose the response that best completes the statement or answers the question.

1. The leader of the Montgomery Improvement Association was
a. E.D. Nixon.
b. Rosa Parks.
c. Martin Luther King, Jr.
d. Jo Ann Robinson.

2. Which of the following was NOT a tactic utilized by black protesters in Montgomery, Alabama?
a. Economic boycott.
b. Circulation of leaflets promoting participation in the protest.
c. Mass civil disobedience.
d. Physical violence and threatening rhetoric.

3. Which of the following did NOT occur during the Truman administration in respect to civil rights?
a. Legislation introduced to make segregated housing illegal.
b. Executive order issued barring segregation in the armed forces.
c. Creation of the President's Committee on Civil Rights.
d. *To Secure These Rights* published in 1947.

4. Which of the following groups represented the backbone of the membership increases in the NAACP during World War II?
a. Educated black professionals.
b. Poor, rural black farmers.
c. Working-class black women.
d. Working and middle-class urban blacks.

5. Black jazz musicians in the forties revolted by expressing their more complex musical visions through
a. hip-hop.
b. bebop.
c. rockabilly.
d. rhythm and blues.

6. Approximately what percentage of eligible Southern black people voted in the late 1940s?
a. Fifty percent
b. One hundred percent
c. Ten percent
d. Twenty-five percent

7. The victory in *Brown v. Board of Education* was limited by the second Brown ruling, which:
a. assigned responsibility for desegregation plans to local school boards.
b. allowed a ten-year period to desegregate.
c. limited the federal funds available to implement desegregation.
d. permitted school boards to reject the decision and counter the suit.

8. The first test case for state versus federal power amidst the controversy over school integration was in
a. Little Rock, Arkansas.
b. Greensboro, North Carolina.
c. Jackson, Mississippi.
d. Montgomery, Alabama.

9. Martin Luther King, Jr. was inspired by this American theologian's social Christianity:
a. Billy Graham.
b. Norman Vincent Peale.
c. Walter Rauschenbusch.
d. Ralph Albernathy.

10. Greensboro, NC, Nashville, TN, and Atlanta, GA were the sites of this particular strategy of the civil rights movement:
a. The Freedom Rides.
b. Voter registration drives to increase the numbers of black voters.
c. Mass marches in southern cities to defeat segregation.
d. Sit-ins at lunch counters, department stores, and restaurants to protest discrimination.

11. Which of the following statements about the Student Nonviolent Coordinating Committee (SNCC) is NOT true?
a. They emphasized fighting segregation through direct confrontation.
b. The organization was hierarchical, adhering to a distinct bureaucratic structure.
c. They stressed spontaneity and improvisation.
d. Three-quarters of the first fieldworkers were less than twenty-two years old.

12. The Albany Movement was first formed as a coalition of activists from these two groups:
a. NAACP and SCLC.
b. CORE and SNCC.
c. SNCC and NAACP.
d. SCLC and CORE.

13. The Birmingham campaign resulted in all of the following EXCEPT
a. increased black voter registration.
b. the death of four young girls in a Baptist Church bombing.
c. the black unemployed and working poor joined the protest.
d. army troops were used to maintain order.

14. Which one of the following was NOT part of the Civil Rights Act of 1964?
a. Discrimination outlawed in employment.
b. Financial aid awarded to communities desegregating their schools.
c. The creation of the Equal Employment Opportunities Commission.
d. The elimination of literacy tests for voter registration.

15. The Freedom Summer activists concentrated on this southern state since it had the lowest number of registered African American voters:
a. Louisiana.
b. Alabama.
c. Mississippi.
d. South Carolina.

16. Malcolm X's abandoned his black separatist views after
a. he made a pilgrimage to Mecca.
b. an assassination attempt on his life.
c. the Civil Rights Act of 1964 was passed.
d. breaking with the Nation of Islam.

17. "Bloody Sunday" was part of the
a. Freedom Summer.
b. Selma campaign.
c. Birmingham campaign.
d. March on Washington.

18. *Braceros* were
a. Mexicans who swam across the Rio Grande River to enter the United States illegally.
b. Temporary agricultural and railroad workers brought to work in the United States during World War II.
c. Mexican American veterans of World War II.
d. Children born of illegal Mexican immigrants in the United States.

19. The Jones Act of 1917 granted United States citizenship to
a. Puerto Ricans.
b. Issei.
c. Native Americans.
d. Mexicans.

20. The Supreme Court decision in *United States v. Wheeler*
a. deemed that separate law schools must be equal.
b. proclaimed the illegality of the segregation of Mexican Americans.
c. reasserted the unique and limited sovereignty of Indian tribes.
d. ended the exclusion of Mexican Americans from Texas jury lists.

Completion: Insert the correct word or phrase to complete the following statements:

1. The 1954 Supreme Court decision in _____ declared that "separate but equal" schools for children of different races were unconstitutional.

2. The formation of the civil rights group _____ in 1942, which advocated non-violent civil disobedience, was an offshoot of the Christian pacifist Fellowship of Reconciliation (FOR).

3. In 1957 Martin Luther King Jr. along with Bayard Rustin of the War Resister's League and other aides brought together nearly 100 black ministers to found the _____.

4. With an emphasis on fighting segregation through direct confrontation, mass action, and civil disobedience, the _____ was founded in 1960 drawing heavily on younger activists and college students.

5. In Albany, a small city in southwest Georgia, activists from SNCC and NAACP, and other local groups formed a coalition of black citizens known as _____ that utilized non-violent civil disobedience in pursuit of voting rights and the integration of public facilities.

6. On July 2, 1964, Lyndon Johnson signed the _____, federal legislation that outlawed discrimination in public accommodations and employment on the basis of race, skin color, sex, religion, or national origin

7. Following the passing of the Civil Rights Act of 1964, a coalition of workers led by SNCC launched the _____ project, an ambitious effort to register black voters in rural Mississippi.

8. The Black Nationalist religious movement the _____ (NOI) which emphasized self-sufficiency, self-help, and separation from white society was founded in depression-era Detroit by Elijah Muhammad.

9. The _____ of 1965 overturned a variety of practices by which states systematically denied voter registration to minorities.

10. Winning the Nobel Peace Prize in 1950, _____ declined an appointment as undersecretary of state because he did not want to subject his family to the segregation laws of Washington, D.C.

True/False: Indicate whether the following statements are true or false.

1. Congressmen from the former Confederate States signed the "Southern Manifesto" in 1956, urging their states to refuse compliance with desegregation. (T/F)

2. The state of California passed a law in 1946 allowing the confiscation of properties owned by Japanese American, defeating the Japanese American Citizens League's efforts to prohibit such acts. (T/F)

3. The Civil Rights Act of 1964 was signed by then-President Lyndon Baines Johnson, prohibiting discrimination of race, color, religion, sex, or national origin. (T/F)

4. Malcolm X was assassinated on February 21, 1965, in front of the Montgomery Alabama courthouse. (T/F)

5. "Operation Wetback" was launched in 1954 in an effort to curb the undocumented immigrants to the United States from Puerto Rico. (T/F)

Map Questions: Refer to the maps and accompanying information presented in the chapter to answer the following questions.

1. Compare and contrast: which states had the lowest percentage of registered black voters in 1960? Which state had the highest in 1960? Which state had the lowest percentage of registered black voters in 1971? Which state had the highest in 1971? (Map 28-2)

2. On the map below, identify by city the key battlegrounds in the civil rights movement, the specific events that unfolded there and the dates they took place. (Map 28-1)

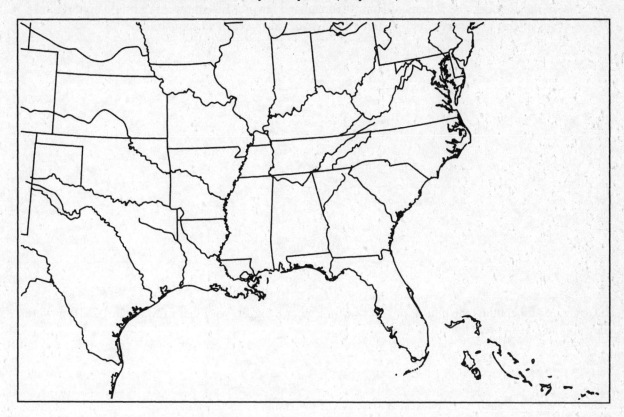

Short Answer Essay

1. Compare the attitudes and actions of Harry Truman and Dwight Eisenhower regarding civil rights. What advancements in the area of civil rights were made during each administration?

2. Compare and contrast the philosophy of Martin Luther King, Jr. with that of Malcolm X. How were they similar? How were they different?

3. Outline the issues and strategies followed by other minorities from 1945 to 1965 who were inspired by the black civil rights movement.

Extended Essay

1. Explain how the various civil rights organizations that formed after World War II, such as the CORE, SCLC, SNCC, and the Albany movement, were instrumental to the success of the movement. What strategies or tactics did they use and how successful were those strategies?

2. Trace the successes and failures of the civil rights movement from the Montgomery Bus Boycott to the Voting Rights Act of 1965. What legal and institutional impact did the movement have on American life and how did it change American culture and politics?

ANSWER KEY

Multiple Choice
1. c (762)
2. d (762)
3. a (763)
4. d (764)
5. b (764)
6. c (765)
7. a (766)
8. a (766)
9. c (768)
10. d (768-769)
11. b (770)
12. c (773)
13. a (774-775)
14. d (776)
15. c (777)
16. a (779)
17. b (781)
18. b (782)
19. a (783)
20. c (784)

Completion
1. *Brown v. Board of Education* (766)
2. Congress of Racial Equality (764)
3. Southern Christian Leadership Conference (768)
4. Student Nonviolent Coordinating Committee (770)
5. the Albany Movement (773)
6. Civil Rights Act of 1964 (776)
7. Freedom Rides (771)
8. Nation of Islam (778)
9. Voting Rights Act (781)
10. Ralph Bunche (764)

True/False
1. T (766)
2. F (785-786)
3. T (776)
4. F (779)
5. F (782)

Chapter Twenty-Nine - War Abroad, War at Home, 1965–1974

LECTURE NOTES:

Multiple Choice: Choose the response that best completes the statement or answers the question.

1. The 1962 Port Huron Statement
a. called for the creation of civilian review boards to check police power.
b. defined Students for a Democratic Society as a new political movement focused on bringing people out of isolation and into community.
c. designated Uptown, Chicago as a Conservation area under the Urban Renewal Act.
d. was drafted by President Lyndon Baines Johnson.

2. Operation Rolling Thunder was based primarily on the premise that
a. search and destroy missions would eradicate the civilian support network for the Vietcong.
b. gradually intensifying air attacks and continued bombing would exhaust North Vietnam's resources.
c. U.S. ground forces would defeat the Vietcong in South Vietnam.
d. the atomic bomb could be used again, if necessary.

3. The American military deaths due to the war in Vietnam increased by how many per week from 1965 to 1967?
a. 154
b. 215
c. 180
d. 100

4. The free speech movement at the University of Berkeley was first formed to
a. demand a revamping of the college curriculum.
b. protest campus rules that treated students as children instead of adults.
c. protest limitations on political activities on campus.
d. bring attention to the discriminatory hiring practices of the University.

5. This counterculture individual urged young people to "turn on, tune in, and drop out:"
a. Bob Dylan.
b. Mario Savio.
c. Timothy Leary.
d. Janis Joplin.

6. The average age of an American soldier in Vietnam was
a. twenty-six.
b. twenty-one.
c. twenty-five.
d. nineteen.

7. The most innovative and controversial element of Johnson's Office of Economic Opportunity was the
a. Community Action Program.
b. Neighborhood Youth Corps.
c. Volunteers in Service to America.
d. Job Corps.

8. Which one of the following statements is TRUE?
a. Spending on social welfare programs between 1960 and 1974 more than doubled.
b. Most social welfare payments went to help the poor.
c. Urban renewal programs were generally beneficial to poor people.
d. The War on Poverty resulted in unprecedented success.

9. The first major urban riot of 1964-1968 took place in the Watts section of
a. Newark, New Jersey.
b. Detroit, Michigan.
c. Cleveland, Ohio.
d. Los Angeles, California.

10. The 1968 Tet Offensive resulted in all of the following EXCEPT
a. Johnson announcing he would not seek the Democratic Party's nomination.
b. the deaths of 1,600 Americans and 40,000 North Vietnamese and Vietcong.
c. an increase in support for the war at home.
d. a major military victory for the United States.

11. Which one of the following is NOT correctly matched to the group it represents?
a. SDS/Students for a Democratic Society
b. GLF/Gay Liberation Front
c. AIM/Asian Independence Movement
d. NOW/National Organization for Women

12. Which of the following statements about the Black Power movement is NOT true?
a. Its key tenets included self-determination and self-sufficiency.
b. It advocated assimilation into white society in order to gain political influence.
c. The most enduring component of the movement was cultural nationalism.
d. It promoted self-esteem by affirming the heritage of African peoples.

13. The Redstockings Manifesto of 1969
a. expressed "the personal is political."
b. called for the creation of a Latina feminist movement.
c. proclaimed women were "exploited as sex objects, breeders, domestic servants, and cheap labor."
d. touched off a new movement for gay liberation.

14. One of the most popular and visible media expressions of Chicano nationalism in the 1960s was the
a. mural.
b. flag.
c. music.
d. television show.

15. United States support of Philippine dictator Ferdinand Marcos was protested by
a. the Black Panthers.
b. Asian Americans.
c. Chicanos.
d. American Indians.

16. The great increase in war protests nationwide, culminating in the tragedies at Kent State and Jackson State, emerged in response to this policy decision:
a. Operation Rolling Thunder.
b. the My Lai Massacre.
c. the Tet Offensive.
d. the invasion of Cambodia.

17. Ping-pong diplomacy symbolized the dramatic changes Nixon made in U.S. policy toward
a. North Vietnam.
b. the Soviet Union.
c. the People's Republic of China
d. the Middle East.

18. In terms of foreign policy, Nixon did all of the following EXCEPT
a. flew to Beijing to meet with the Chinese foreign minister.
b. sold $1 billion dollars of grain to the Soviets.
c. accelerated the delivery of arms to foreign dictators.
d. secured peace in the Middle East.

19. The "Saturday Night Massacre" was the name given to
a. Nixon ordering special prosecutor Archibald Cox fired.
b. Nixon's negative political campaign against George McGovern.
c. The round-up of the intruders who wire tapped the Democratic National Committee headquarters.
d. Bob Woodward and Carl Bernstein breaking the Watergate story in the Washington Post.

20. Which of the following statements is TRUE?
a. Nixon was successful in suppressing the Pentagon Papers.
b. Nixon was the second president in American history to be impeached.
c. Nixon was the first president in American history to resign from office.
d. Nixon was not directly involved with the Watergate break-in.

Completion: Insert the correct word or phrase to complete the following statements:

1. The leading student organization of the New Left of the early and mid-1960s promoted a "culture of life" in the face of "the culture of death" symbolized by the war in Vietnam was; this organization was

_____

2. In response to North Vietnamese torpedo boat attacks on two U.S. destroyers, Lyndon Johnson appealed to Congress to pass the _____ giving him the authority "to take all necessary measures" to defend U.S. armed forces to protect Southeast Asia "against aggression or subversion."

3. The first sign of a new kind of protest movement was the _____ at the University of California at Berkeley in 1964 which stood against the limitation of campus political activities.

4. The new form of community emerging in the 1960s that emphasized alternatives to mainstream values and behaviors known as the_____ embraced communal living, a return to the land, Asian religions, and experimentation with psychedelic drugs.

5. In August 1964 the Economic Opportunity Act launched the _____, a set of programs designed to break the cycle of poverty by providing funds for job training, community development, nutrition, and supplementary education mostly to urban black youths.

6. The key tenets of _____ philosophy emerging after 1965 were that self-help and self determination were the primary means by which African Americans could achieve real economic and political gains.

7. The Native American political activist group known as _____, founded in 1968, used confrontations with the federal government to publicize their case for Indian rights.

8. In 1971 the U.S. Army court-martialed Lt. William L. Cally Jr. for the murder of "at least" 22 Vietnamese civilians during a 1968 search-and-destroy mission subsequently known as the _____.

9. Although a limited measure, the first successful step toward strategic arms control since the onset of the Cold War came with the 1972 _____between the United States and the Soviet Union.

10. The _____ scandal involving attempts to cover up illegal actions taken by administration officials led to the resignation of President Richard Nixon in 1974.

True/False: Indicate whether the following statements are true or false.

1. Michael Harrington argued in his 1962 book, *The Other America* that more than 50 million Americans suffered from poverty. (T/F)

2. The Gay Liberation Front both supported the war in Vietnam and opposed the militant tactics of the Black Panther Party. (T/F)

3. The first successful union of migrant workers was the United Farm Workers spearheaded by Cesar Chavez in 1965. (T/F)

4. The Environmental Protection Agency was created during Richard Nixon's administration. (T/F)

5. The so-called Pentagon Papers exposed the role of Richard Nixon in the Watergate scandal. (T/F)

Map Questions: Refer to the maps and accompanying information presented in the chapter to answer the following questions.

1. Where were campus-based protests centered in the United States when they first began? Where and why did they spread? What other divisions in American society were exposed by the debate over the war in Vietnam? (Map 29-1)

2. After reviewing the map, label the states and cities that experienced the most uprisings between 1965 and 1968. What did rioters take aim at in their communities and what were the main factors behind urban unrest? (Map 29-2)

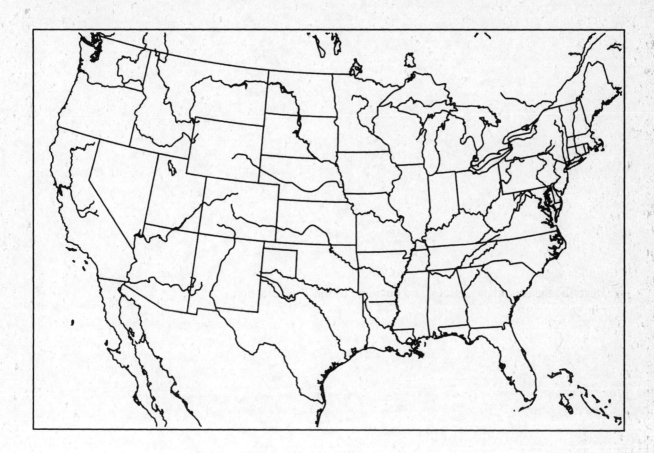

Short Answer Essay

1. Outline the goals of Lyndon Johnson's Great Society. How successful was he in meeting these goals?

2. Describe the candidates, issues, and outcome of the 1968 election.

3. Trace the events in the Watergate case leading up to Nixon's resignation in 1974.

Extended Essay

1. Discuss the events that led up to and contributed to United States involvement in Vietnam. How did Americans respond to the war and what was the result of the war, both politically and emotionally?

2. Discuss the "politics of identity," addressing, specifically, the emergence of various movements and their political activism throughout the 1960s. How did these groups become more "visible" in the 1960s?

ANSWER KEY

Multiple Choice
1. b (792)
2. b (794)
3. a (795)
4. c (796)
5. c (797)
6. d (799)
7. a (801)
8. a (801-803)
9. d (803)
10. c (805)
11. c (811)
12. b (809-810)
13. c (810)
14. a (814)
15. b (816)
16. d (818)
17. c (819)
18. d (819-821)
19. a (822-823)
20. c (823)

Completion
1. Students for a Democratic Society (796)
2. Tonkin Gulf Resolution (793)
3. free speech movement (796)
4. counterculture (797)
5. war on poverty (801)
6. Black Power (809)
7. American Indian Movement (814)
8. My Lai Massacre (819)
9. Strategic Arms Limitation Treaty (820)
10. Watergate (823)

True/False
1. F (801)
2. F (813)
3. T (814)
4. T (820)
5. F (822)

LECTURE NOTES:

Multiple Choice: Choose the response that best completes the statement or answers the question.

1. Conservative voters in Orange County were least likely to support
a. big government.
b. tax cuts.
c. abortion rights.
d. family values.

2. "Stagflation" was characterized by all of the following EXCEPT
a. skyrocketing prices.
b. overproduction.
c. rising unemployment.
d. low economic growth.

3. The Nixon administration responded to OPEC's oil embargo in all of the follow ways EXCEPT
a. ordering a 10 percent reduction in air travel.
b. extending daylight savings time into the winter months.
c. lowering speed limits on interstate highways to 55 miles per hour.
d. creating the Department of Energy in 1973.

4. Sunbelt states were least likely to spend their tax and federal dollars on
a. public housing.
b. strengthening police forces.
c. creating budget surpluses.
d. building roads and sanitation systems.

5. Jimmy Carter offered this as his chief qualification for the presidency:
a. experience as governor of Georgia.
b. "born-again" Christianity.
c. personal integrity.
d. moderate political position.

6. Neighborhood restoration in the 1970s was often accompanied by "gentrification," which
a. created housing for elderly residents of a community.
b. lowered rents in many urban locations.
c. displaced poor residents by more prosperous Americans who craved fashionable old homes.
d. made mortgages more attainable for most buyers.

7. Three Mile Island exposed the problems associated with
a. toxic waste dumping.
b. the use of DDT.
c. damming wetlands for housing development.
d. the use of nuclear power.

8. By 1980, this grew to become the federal government's largest regulatory agency:
a. Community Development Corporation.
b. Environmental Protection Agency.
c. Equal Employment Opportunity Commission.
d. Department of Energy.

9. Political activity in the 1970s is best described as
a. increasingly apathetic.
b. centered around local campaigns and newly organized voluntary associations.
c. focused primarily on national elections and party affiliations.
d. traditional in the sense that no new groups entered the political arena.

10. Which one of the following is NOT an example of the new conservatism?
a. Passage of Proposition 13 in California
b. Popularity of the Moral Majority
c. The STOP ERA campaign
d. Support for *Roe v. Wade*

11. All of the following were increasing trends of the "Me Decade" EXCEPT
a. transcendental meditation.
b. religious cults.
c. decreasing premarital sexual activity.
d. nostalgic and nihilistic popular music.

12. Which one of the following areas proved to be a foreign policy success for Jimmy Carter?
a. Iran
b. Panama
c. Nicaragua
d. El Salvador

13. Which one of the following was NOT a condition of the Camp David Accords?
a. The United States secured a right to oil fields in the region.
b. Israel would return to its approximate borders of 1967.
c. Egypt recognized Israel's right to exist as an independent state.
d. Egypt regained control of the Sinai Peninsula.

14. Presidential Directive 59
a. halted exports of grain and high technology to the USSR.
b. asserted the determination of the United States to protect its interests in the Persian Gulf.
c. allowed the deposed Shah of Iran to enter the United States.
d. guaranteed the production of weapons necessary to win a prolonged nuclear war.

15. The Reagan Administration reduced federal spending in all of the following areas EXCEPT:
a. the arts.
b. education.
c. defense.
d. the environment.

16. By the mid-1980s, the United States became the world's
a. leading creditor.
b. smallest exporter.
c. largest importer
d. biggest debtor.

17. An estimated one-third of the nation's homeless people in the 1980s were
a. alcoholics.
b. formerly discharged mental patients.
c. Vietnam veterans.
d. AIDS victims.

18. The Reagan Doctrine assumed that political instability in the Third World
a. resulted from factors such as poverty or corruption.
b. would resolve itself, without U.S. intervention.
c. was a result of the pernicious influence of the Soviet Union.
d. was a continuation of the "Vietnam syndrome."

19. In 1981, Reagan approved a CIA plan to arm and organize the Contras, who were
a. Salvadorian rebels.   c. Nicaraguan exiles.
b. Sandinista revolutionaries. d. Central American refugees.

20. Between 1985 and 1988, Reagan had four separate summit meetings with this Soviet leader:
a. Mikhail Gorbachev.   c. Yuri Andropov.
b. Leonid Brezhnev.   d. Konstantin Chernenko.

Completion: Insert the correct word or phrase to complete the following statements:

1. The cartel of oil-producing nations in Asia, Africa, and Latin America, _____ gained substantial power over the world economy in the mid- to late-1970s by controlling the production and price of oil.

2. _____, the reduction or removal of government regulations and encouragement of direct competition in many important industries, was considered a successful innovation of the Carter Presidency.

3. _____programs helped to open opportunities in business and education for members of minority groups and women by allowing race and sex to be factors in hiring, the awarding of contracts, and admission into institutions of higher education.

4. The 1973 Supreme Court ruling in _____ disallowed state laws prohibiting abortion during the first trimester of pregnancy while establishing guidelines for abortion in the second and third trimesters.

5. From the French for "easing tension," _____ described the new U.S. relations with China and the Soviet Union in 1972.

6. _____is a complex of deadly pathologies resulting from infection with the human immunodeficiency virus (HIV)

7. _____, the Russian word for "openness," applied to Mikhail Gorbachev's encouragement of new ideas and the easing of political repression in the Soviet Union.

8. President Ronald Reagan's _____, announced in 1983, was aimed at developing sophisticated technologies to defend the U.S. against nuclear missile attack.

9. Russian for "restructuring," _____ applied to Mikhail Gorbachev's efforts to make the soviet economic and political systems more modern, flexible, and innovative.

10. In 1978 the _____ signed by Israel and Egypt set the formal terms for peace in the Middle East. In doing so Egypt became the first Arab country to recognize Israel's right to exist.

True/False: Indicate whether the following statements are true or false.

1. Gerald Ford issued more vetoes of major bills than any other president in the twentieth century. (T/F)

2. In *Roe v. Wade*, the United States Supreme Court allowed state laws to prohibit abortion during the first three months of pregnancy. (T/F)

3. President Reagan's economic policies adhered to "supply-side" theory, which called for cutting taxes to increase consumer activity, with the aim of promoting economic growth. (T/F)

4. The nation's most populous states in the 1970s were California, New York, and Texas, respectively. (T/F)

5. Formed by Rev. Pat Robertson, the Moral Majority was a political lobbying group that advocated tough laws against homosexuality and pornography. (T/F)

Map Questions: Refer to the maps and accompanying information presented in the chapter to answer the following questions.

1. What overall shifts occurred in the United States population between 1970 and 1980? What two events coincided to cause this shift? Where were the highest population gains? Where was the highest concentration of population losses? (Map 30-2)

2. Compare the election results of 1976 (Map 30-3) with those of 1980 (Map 30-4). Shade the states that Carter carried in 1976 that he did not carry in 1980. What was Carter's advantage in 1976? What was his major disadvantage in 1980? What consequences did both of the elections have for Congress?

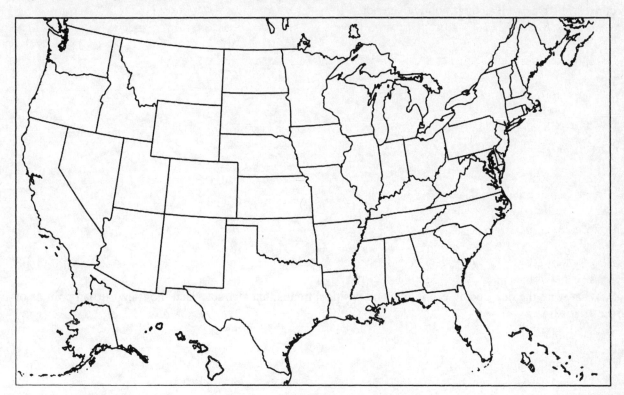

Short Answer Essay

1. Describe the new conservatism, identifying those groups who contributed to the growth of conservatism as well as their political agenda.

2. What were the new social, economic, and political trends that characterized the "new" urban politics of the 1970s?

3. What was the Iran-Contra scandal and what did it demonstrate to the American people?

Extended Essay

1. Evaluate the presidency of Jimmy Carter. Where was he most successful? Where did he fail? What shifts in foreign policy occurred during Carter's administration and what are the consequences of those shifts today?

2. Describe the central philosophy and assumptions behind Reaganomics. How was this economic theory implemented? Address both the positive and negative consequences of Reaganomics.

ANSWER KEY

Multiple Choice
1. c (832)
2. b (833)
3. d (833)
4. a (836)
5. c (837)
6. c (839)
7. d (839)
8. b (840)
9. b (837)
10. d (841-842)
11. c (843)
12. b (846)
13. a (846)
14. d (847)
15. c (850)
16. d (852)
17. b (855-856)
18. c (856)
19. c (857)
20. a (858)

Completion
1. OPEC (833)
2. Deregulation (837)
3. Affirmative Action (838)
4. *Roe v. Wade* (842)
5. détente (847)
6. Acquired Immune Deficiency Syndrome - AIDS (855)
7. *Glasnost* (857)
8. Strategic Defense Initiative (856)
9. *perestroika* (857)
10. Camp David Accords (846)

True/False
1. T (836)
2. F (842)
3. T (849-851)
4. T (835)
5. F (841)

Chapter Thirty-One - Toward a Transnational America, since 1988

LECTURE NOTES:

Multiple Choice: Choose the response that best completes the statement or answers the question.

1. Which one of the following statements is NOT true?
a. More than 50,000 people worked at the World Trade Center.
b. The majority of Hispanic New Yorkers in 2001 were Cubans and Puerto Ricans.
c. The World Trade Center was home to multinational businesses from Latin America, Asia, Africa, and Europe.
d. Citizens from eighty-one nations perished in the terrorist attacks of September 11, 2001.

2. The most dramatic event in the collapse of Communism occurred in 1989 in
a. Romania.
b. Czechoslovakia.
c. East Germany.
d. Poland.

3. The first concern of the United States in response to Iraq's 2000 invasion of Kuwait was
a. dislodging Saddam Hussein.
b. that Iraq may also attack Saudi Arabia.
c. to avoid military action by tightening sanctions.
d. to keep deployment of forces relatively low.

4. The Dayton Accords
a. promised security for Israelis and self-rule for Palestinians.
b. formally ended the war in Iraq.
c. authorized NATO air strikes in Kosovo.
d. called for a federated, multiethnic state of Bosnia.

5. The goal of the Gramm-Rudman Act was
a. to bailout the savings and loan industry.
b. a balanced federal budget.
c. ending federal welfare programs.
d. promoting free trade.

6. Which one of the following slashed tariffs on goods and phased out import quotas?
a. World Trade Organization.
b. North Atlantic Free Trade Agreement.
c. General Agreement on Tariffs and Trade.
d. Gramm-Rudman Act.

7. One of the common business strategies during the 1990s for increasing profit levels or defeating negative trends was
a. outsourcing.
b. expanding.
c. downsizing.
d. relocating.

8. By 2000, one-third of the work force of "Silicon Valley" was employed in
a. fruit and vegetable processing.
b. heavy industry.
c. the service sector.
d. electronics and high-tech firms.

9. The Immigration Reform and Control Act of 1986
a. abolished discriminatory national origins quotas from the 1920s.
b. offered amnesty to all undocumented workers who had entered the country since 1982.
c. limited immigration from Latin America.
d. deported illegal immigrants back to their home country.

10. The largest Asian ethnicity in the United States in the 1990s was
a. Japanese.
b. Vietnamese.
c. Chinese.
d. Indian.

11. The 1992 Los Angeles riot ignited over the issue of
a. police brutality.
b. racial profiling.
c. school integration.
d. ethnic tensions.

12. Timothy McVeigh was executed for his involvement in the
a. Oklahoma City bombing.
b. Branch Davidian siege.
c. Columbine High School shootings.
d. 1993 bombing of the World Trade Center.

13. Proposition 187 called for
a. a greater focus on multiculturalism in schools.
b. a constitutional ban of same-sex marriage.
c. an end to embryonic stem cell research.
d. making all undocumented aliens ineligible for welfare services.

14. The first state to recognize same-sex, civil unions was
a. California.
b. New York.
c. Massachusetts.
d. Vermont.

15. The "Contract with America" proposed cuts in all of the following areas EXCEPT
a. military spending.
b. federal welfare programs.
c. taxes.
d. federal regulatory power in the environment.

16. The four articles of impeachment brought by the House Judiciary Committee in 1998 charged Clinton with all of the following EXCEPT
a. witness tampering.
b. perjury.
c. obstruction of justice.
d. adultery.

17. Which one of the following statements does NOT accurately describe the presidential election of 2000?
a. The winner of the popular vote did not win the Electoral College vote.
b. The Democrats had the first Jewish candidate for vice-president.
c. There were no third party candidates involved in the race.
d. It was the first presidential election to be decided by a decision of the Supreme Court.

18. The Triad is made up of
a. Canada, Mexico, and the United States.
b. Japan, North America, and Europe.
c. North Korea, Iraq, and Iran.
d. North America, Europe, and China.

19. The most distinctive characteristic of the current trend towards "globalization" is the
a. rate of growth.
b. volume of revenues from multinational corporations.
c. movement towards a single international market.
d. existence of well-organized transnational economies.

20. In the wake of the September 11, 2001 attacks on the World Trade Center and the Pentagon, all of the following occurred EXCEPT
a. U.S. air strikes were ordered in Afghanistan
b. Osama Bin Laden was brought before the International War Crimes Tribunal.
c. the Department of Homeland Security was created.
d. NATO invoked the mutual defense clause for the first time ever.

Completion: Insert the correct word or phrase to complete the following statements:

1. _____, a southeastern European nation that split off from Yugoslavia, became the site of a bitter civil and religious war, requiring NATO and U.S. intervention in the 1990s.

2. The U.S. military campaign _____ was launched January 16, 1991, to remove invading Iraqi forces from Kuwait.

3. The _____ law mandated automatic spending cuts if the government failed to meet fixed deficit reduction goals leading to balanced budget by 1991.

4. The _____ was reached in 1993 by Canada, Mexico, and the United States to substantially reduce barriers to trade, thereby easing the international flow of goods, services, and investments.

5. The system of interconnected computers and servers known as the _____ allows for the exchange of e-mail, posting of web sites, and other means of instant communication.

6. The _____ sets standards and practices for global trade, and was the focus of international protests over world economic policy in the late 1990s.

7. _____ is a controversial movement that emphasizes the unique attributes and achievements of marginal groups and recent immigrants.

8. Adopted by popular vote in California in 1994, _____ cuts off state-funded health and education benefits to undocumented or illegal immigrants.

9. The _____scandal involved an Arkansas real estate development in which Bill and Hillary Clinton were investors: although several fraud convictions resulted from investigations into the development project, no evidence was found that implicated the Clintons in any wrongdoing.

10. The _____ specified that gay couples would be ineligible for spousal benefits provided by federal law.

True/False: Indicate whether the following statements are true or false.

1. The Persian Gulf War was initiated by President George H.W. Bush in response to Iraq's invasion of Kuwait. (T/F)

2. NAFTA, the North American Free Trade Agreement, was rejected by Congress in November 1993. (T/F)

3. Silicon Valley is the region of California that holds the nation's largest concentration of industrial firms. (T/F)

4. The 2000 presidential election was the closest election in United States history and the first to be decided by the Supreme Court. (T/F)

5. According to the 2000 U.S. Census, the largest Hispanic group in the United States was Puerto Rican. (T/F)

Map Questions: Refer to the maps and accompanying information presented in the chapter to answer the following questions.

1. After reviewing the chart on page 875, "Continent of Birth for Immigrants 1990-2000," identify, from highest percent to lowest, where most immigrants to the United States during this period were coming from. What factors account for these trends and how do they differ from previous patterns of immigration in the twentieth century?

Short Answer Essay

1. What two major trade agreements did President Clinton push through Congress? What were the positive and negative consequences of these actions?

2. What led to the creation of an "electronic culture" and how has the influence of technology, such as in television, become more powerful in American culture?

3. What were the major divisions in American society at the end of the twentieth century and what conditions contributed to these divisions?

Extended Essay

1. What led to the collapse of Communism and the end of the Cold War? What region has become the new focus of mounting tensions and the basis for international affairs and why? Address, for example, U.S. military involvement in the Middle East and in the Balkans in the 1990s

2. Evaluate the presidency of Bill Clinton. How are his domestic and foreign policies different from those Republican presidents who preceded him? How are they similar? What was the impact of the scandals that plagued his presidency?

ANSWER KEY

Multiple Choice
1. b (866-867)
2. c (867)
3. b (868)
4. d (870)
5. b (871)
6. c (872)
7. c (872)
8. d (873)
9. b (876)
10. c (877)
11. a (878)
12. a (880-881)
13. d (882)
14. d (883)

15. a (882)
16. d (885)
17. c (885-886)
18. b (887)
19. b (887)
20. b (888-890)

Completion
1. Bosnia (870)
2. Operation Desert Storm (868)
3. Gramm-Rudman (871)
4. North American Free Trade Agreement (NAFTA) (872)

5. Internet (873)
6. World Trade Organization (WTO) (872)
7. Multiculturalism (880)
8. Proposition 187 (882)
9. Whitewater (884)
10. Defense of Marriage Act (883)

True/False
1. T (869)
2. F (872)
3. F (873)
4. T (885-886)
5. F (876)